Whet

Short Erotic Tales
of
Otherworldly Desire

~ * ~ * ~

by jd romann

~ * ~ * ~

The stories in this book (some in different versions) have appeared in the following places:

- Best Gay Love Stories 2006, edited by Nick Street
- Best Gay Love Stories 2005, edited by Nick Street
- Friction 7: Best Gay Erotic Fiction, edited by Jesse Grant
- Wet Nightmares, Wet Dreams, edited by Michael Huxley
- VelvetMafia.com, edited by Sean Meriwether
- MindCaviar.com, edited by Jamie Joy Gatto

www.JDRomann.com

JDRomann@hotmail.com

Cover Design: SelfPubBookCovers.com/Island

Contents

Jump

Two men. Neighboring balconies. Each man stands on a jutting slab of concrete suspended in space. One's face known to millions. Unmistakable dark mane, now tangled and damp. Bare-chested and barefoot despite the snow, Axis stares down toward the pavement seventeen stories below.

The other man unknown yet unforgettable. Erie packs his brawn into brown leather. Barbed-wire bracelet, close-cropped hair white-blonde, pressed into shadows.

Axis rests his weight on the railing and lifts a foot, hoists himself up.

Erie says, "What a cliché that would be."

Axis looks up. Reveals his unshaven face in the spilled hotel room light. Steps back, away from the railing, away from the man's gaze. He body hugs himself, hands wedged in opposite armpits. His unbelted jeans sag at the waist. "Insomnia," he rasps. He retreats inside. The night sucks the curtain out through the open door.

The blonde man throbs in Axis's head. Lodges in his peripheral vision, lingering like the spot after a hot stage light. He waits for it to burst with migraine explosion, then fade. But it hovers. Silent irritant. He switches the room lights off and paces. Ignores congealing room-service food. Steps back outside. Puts a cigarette to his lips.

A lighter scratches to life in the nearby darkness. A small flame illuminates the blonde man.

Axis leans out over the wide space between their balconies, torso balanced on the rail, cold steel pressed to skin. Erie lights his cigarette across the void. "You'll die of hypothermia before you have to jump, dressed like that. Or maybe I should say, undressed."

Axis settles back on his bare feet. "Can't feel it. Look." He extinguishes the cigarette on the inside of his scarred wrist. "I'm numb. Can't feel anything." His voice fades in and out, a car radio driving through mountains. The cigarette hisses on crusted snow when he drops it. "You didn't tell me to stop," he says.

Erie lights his own cigarette. Unzips his jacket and presses the burning tip against a pink, pierced nipple. The odor of their singed flesh mingles, famous and anonymous, pierces city winter's damp cloud of smell. Curling smoke rises with breath's steam.

"Don't." Axis's voice breaks.

"See?" The cigarette flutters down, trailing embers, like burning feathers from a fallen angel's wings. "You can feel."

Car tires slush on the street below, seeking traction. "You know who I am?" But it is not a question.

"Axis." Millions have screamed his name, but never has a voice contained a secret in its sibilance. "Fallen rock star." The hiss is neither malevolent nor sympathetic, just matter of fact.

Axis retreats, wedged into the balcony's far corner. "No camera?"

"Not my kind of souvenir."

"What, then? Autograph? My hair? My shirt?" The jagged shards of his voice carve bitterness into his words.

"To fuck you."

"Yeah, you and half the planet." Axis looks down over the railing, yearning, but the other man's stare pulls him back.

"No. They want you to fuck them. To fill their emptiness."

"What's the difference?"

Erie places one hand on the railing and vaults through space to Axis's balcony. The space is too wide, he moves too slowly. He falters when he lands—or does he—tumbling to Axis's feet. Axis kneels, hands outstretched. "You okay? How did you—? You could have—"

Erie grips the back of Axis's neck, pulls him down into a hard kiss. Presses Axis's cold fingers to his crotch, a leather bulge that will burst its hide. Axis doesn't protest or return the kiss. A stranger's tongue explores his slack and open mouth. Muffled sound and scattered light leak through the barricade of balcony walls.

Erie places his other hand on the fly of Axis's worn jeans, feels only buttons and the stiff seam. Axis flinches, pulls out of the kiss.

"You've never been fucked." Erie's hand on denim strokes. No response. He undoes Axis's fly, one button slow popped at a time, single-handed, still pressing Axis's hand to his own erection. Erie's hand creeps into Axis's open jeans.

"Don't."

Erie finds what he's looking for. "Broken wing?"

"I can't—"

"—fuck."

"—sing." A passing siren swallows Axis's graveled voice.

Erie rolls Axis onto his back, straddles him. Axis doesn't resist, his body as limp as his cock. They leave a warped snow angel smudged into the meager snow beside them.

Erie strips him. Axis lies naked on the cold concrete. His cock recoils into dense, dark pubic hair.

"I'm so tired," Axis whispers.

Erie unhitches his own erection. He leaves the waist of his pants snapped closed but opens the zipper. A big man, his proportionate cock thrusts white out of dark leather. Erie rubs his cock on the arch of Axis's foot. Along his ankle, calf, knee, thigh. Leather creaks, sticks on Axis's frozen flesh. Erie inches his way up Axis's body, velvet cock stroke followed by zipper's scratch, until his knees are in Axis's armpits.

Axis watches snowflakes melt on his outstretched palm.

Erie's cock rises up Axis's neck, his chin, rests at his mouth. Nudges apart the lips—they graze microphones like this as he croons and purrs immortal sound. Pries open the teeth. Eases inside. Axis allows the trespass. Erie pushes back, slipping along the tongue, and back, kissing vocal cords that have charmed the world, and back. The shaft down his insured throat impales Axis against the concrete. Both men are still. Cock blood pulses. Axis's nostrils flare.

"You're dead," Erie says. "I'll fill your body. I'll make you feel."

Axis passes out.

He wakes in a hot bath. Steam rises from dense bubbles. His skin is pickled, angry red from a close shave and scrubbing, his hair washed and combed. A bandage covers his cigarette burn. Erie sits under and behind him, Erie's hard cock wedged against Axis's ass crack. Water drips from the faucet, plinking into the full tub.

Erie holds Axis's slim hips, slides him up and down. Slow, slippery friction. Axis's slight body slips easily in the perfumed soap. Water laps over the tub's side, sprays the floor.

Axis sputters and thrashes, whirling to face him.

They both stand, dripping. Axis's cock dangles, Erie's threatens. Erie steps out of the tub. Without drying off, he leaves the bathroom.

Axis, wrapped in a towel, follows his wet footprints in the silent darkness. Erie stretches out on the bed, glistening wet, eyes closed. Hairless: pubic, body, face. Only scant eyebrows and shorn prickles on his head. White and slick as an albino sea creature. His hard cock insists. The latex encasement heightens its menace, as if to touch it directly will turn a mortal to salt.

Axis approaches the bed. Erie reaches out, snags the towel and tugs. The white cloth slips to Axis's feet, material coiled at a statue's base. Erie clutches the limp cock. "Sex symbol," he says, opening his eyes.

"My voice." Axis touches his throat.

"Shrouded. Not lost."

"I don't know when I last slept or ate." Pill bottles and paraphernalia litter the nightstand.

"Or fucked."

"Men have wanted me before." Axis's shrapnelled words disintegrate.

"But you never let them. You've closed yourself off." Erie guides him up onto the bed, half lifting him, until Axis straddles him. Up on his knees, Axis's balls hang, empty as a purgatory soul. "You're the dried up river bed below a concrete dam."

Erie guides Axis over his own greased cock, connects. Axis gasps. Erie holds Axis's hips, eases him down. Axis trembles and moans. His palms lay flat on Erie's abdomen, then clench into fists. Erie works his weight, now raising him, now lowering him farther, until Axis has taken in all of him. Axis shakes and bucks. "I can't, I…" He sags forward.

Erie rolls them over without separating. Erie's cock pins Axis on his back. Between his spread legs, Erie fucks him. "Feel," he says. He pulls out his full extension after each thrust. "Feel me. Feel it."

The cock is an unfurling angel's wing dipped in hot tar. Feathers that susurrate and serrate. Muscle that whispers and pounds. Softness aflame. Exquisite agony. Blissful, hallucinogenic agony. The mattress dances off the box spring and nudges the nightstand. Medicine bottles tumble to the floor. As Axis moans, his balls and cock fill. They are no sooner engorged than Axis shudders and comes. He floods his navel. He touches this now rare juice, astonished.

Erie climbs off him. Axis cries out at the sudden emptiness.

Erie rolls him onto his side, enters him from behind. Erie reaches around to hold his sticky cock, and Axis falls asleep. Erie cocoons the blankets around them.

Whenever Axis stirs, Erie swells inside him before he wakes, fucks him back to sleep, cradles him as he penetrates. The thorned bracelet marries each caress to a delicate scratch.

Not until dawn does Erie stand, push Axis to his knees and push himself again down Axis's throat, no latex, and—finally—comes himself. Axis swallows, and swallows. Tastes fruit punch and gasoline. Stalagmite-ice and blue-hot solder. He smells ash and pink cotton candy. Erie's sound as he comes is silent but percussive, an echoing cave at the center of the earth. The sound of all souls yearning. Of eternity.

Only Erie's hands in Axis's hair keep him upright while Erie floods him, fills up what he has emptied. Erie uses and fills every inch of him. Erie's orgasm is endless, and Axis, too, comes, without touch, his hands behind Erie's knees, hanging on. Impossible that he should have anything left to come, he comes in mercury and opal dew and rainforest rain. Wave after wave, the dam bursts.

Axis hums. Sweetly hums, a lace chandelier in a breeze, around Erie's cock. And Erie laughs.

Erie raises him and brings him to his breast. Sucking Erie's nipple, Axis notices the burning cigarette had left no mark.

~ * ~ * ~

Awakening alone, a fading ray of sunlight slashes Axis's face. He'd slept through the day. Dried sex juice crackles on his blood-mapped skin. As if a clawed bird danced on Axis's body, a network of fine scratches mark the trail of Erie's bracelet. The sheets are shredded, and singed in places, as though a shower of matches had flared and snuffed out.

Axis stretches, snagging the sheets and scratching his forehead with Erie's barbed-wire bracelet. He stares at the gift on his wrist. There is no join, no clasp.

His tenderized insides pulse. He walks awkwardly, a toddler taking his first steps. He calls Erie's name. The curtain billows out of the empty room. He devours whatever food he can find, leaving a trail of plastic wrappers, juice cans, fruit skins. His cock blossoms toward the murky sunset as he hums a childhood hymn, crystal notes dancing.

The thorned bracelet will become Axis's new trademark, always on his wrist. It's a pain in the ass, never lets him forget it's there. He knows what he would lose by cutting it off.

Sometimes when he is melancholy, alone despite the millions who deify him, he will dream. He is on all fours. Fluttering softness envelops him, but behind him, inside him, is hardness. He dreads the visitation as much as he requires it, he spreads himself even as he resists the entry, he bows down, he pulls away but thrusts back. Heated copper blazes inside him and he comes hard as he wakens. An odor of smelters and bubble gum lingers, and he finds a feather. His bracelet has ripped the down pillow, but the feather is brown, with a stiff white spine.

He keeps the plain feathers to brush himself with. They are the breath of an angel on his cock as he kneels, naked on a high balcony when his voice breaks into static, and he sings his reverence, scratching his thigh with the bracelet as he strokes himself, crying noyesyesno as if it is one word.

The scorch of the blessing intensifies each time, and his pubic hair, and then his underarm and belly hair, turns downy. But if he can sing yesyesyesyes to the scalding love he beckons, Erie will alight and consecrate his throat. Axis will taste maple syrup in petroleum, and he will sing purely again, for a time, in rapture.

Tail

The lovers fish him out of the frigid sea. The drowned man is as heavy and stiff as a granite statue. The two men hoist him onto the teak deck. Their hands go numb from holding his frozen body. They lay him down carefully, afraid he'll shatter like an ice sculpture.

Dewey kneels and listens at his mouth. "He's breathing."

"Too bad. No mouth to mouth." Eddie wisecracks because he's relieved—he's not sure they know how to rescue a human ice cube.

Dewey surveys their larger-than-life catch. The drowned man's skin is blue-tinged. His frost-covered hair and beard twinkle in the sunset, as if he wears the constellations in his shaggy, black locks. He trails seaweed, his body festooned with slimy ribbons. Slick algae coats his fingernails.

"Jesus, there's nothing around for miles. How'd he get here?" Eddie scans the bobbing, dusk-blue horizon in all directions. The ocean is calm, and the boat rocks gently under his feet.

"Dunno. Shipwreck, I guess."

"Shipwrecks take storms." Eddie jams his fists in his parka. "Hasn't been wind or a cloud in days."

Dewey knows this. They have drifted in the doldrums, unconcerned, their lovemaking as slow and languorous as the unhurried, directionless tide. Below deck, they generate their own heat. Their bodies slap together like the gentle slaps of the waves on the hull, a dull knocking that startles them in the absolute quiet. Dewey mistakes the low creaking of swollen timbers for a voice. Eddie berates him as he goes above board to put his lover's mind at rest, but adores him for the fertile imagination that nourishes bedroom fantasy. Good thing Eddie humors him, else he would never have spied this shipwrecked soul floating past the *Neptune III*.

A fresh breeze now teases Dewey's coat and the lashed sails. "He's a crusty old salt, that's for sure. Looks like he could steer a pirate ship through a hurricane."

"Yeah, Christ, what a get-up. Like someone needs to tell him it's a new century."

"Come on, fashion queen, better dry him off and get him a blanket."

They strip him. The ill-fitting outfit falls apart in their hands.

They stand and gawk, their mortal minds struggling to explain a creature this magnificent. The man is chiseled marble, fallen off his pedestal. He is a temple shrine. He has risen from an ancient, treasure-laden shipwreck, a divinity that sank on his travels to another realm. Humans have been sacrificed at his ivory feet. This dredged cargo should not be prone before them. They should

11

be prostrate before him in lustful homage, a pair of supplicants beseeching fulfillment of their desires. But they are not god-fearing. They worship the male body, and they have hooked this icon of their religion. He is not an archaic carving, but frozen flesh. Alive.

His cock is as stiff, blue, and impressive as the rest of him. They stare, touching hands. Eddie whistles low. "Jesus. We found the fucking Titanic."

"You'd think it'd shrivel in the cold," Dewey whispers in reverent awe.

"It's bigger than our damn anchor."

"Just don't bump it. It might chip off. Like those castrated statues."

"Some memento of our trip that would be. Maybe they could surgically attach it to me." Eddie's dick is big enough to feature heavily in local mythology, as well as a few porn flicks, but he feels puny in comparison to this mighty godhead. "It's frozen. It'll stay preserved, right?"

Dewey shakes his head, snaps out of this cult-like stupor. "Let's get him inside."

They towel him down, Eddie taking great care to dry the man's awesome cock. Scales cover the towel. Eddie grimaces. "Yuck. What's that stuff?"

"Must have been in an oil slick when his boat went down."

"Smells funny, that's for damn sure."

"There something strange about all this. I'm not sure I like it."

"You and your superstitions. What's there not to like about snagging a nuclear submarine? Our friends'll never believe us." Eddie stretches his arms wide. "It was *this* big."

They lift the rescued colossus. He is a slick totem pole and slips in their grip. His rigid body will not bend. They wedge him into the cabin, like sliding a frozen pizza into an oven.

They lay him on the V-berth. The head of the bed is a mere point at the prow of the ship, but the bed widens as the ship does, so that the foot of the bed is expansive. The boat is small, but the mattress is big. Recreation is limited at open sea, and the lovers don't want their style cramped. They sail for privacy. They rock and cry out with abandon. They don't yet know what their wails have summoned.

The man's arms cross over his chest, a stern, disapproving deity. His forearms push up his pecs, and his fingers brush alert, inky nipples. He seems to be offering his breasts. Eddie appraises him. "Man, he's got big titties."

"He's got big everything."

"Yeah, but he spends more time on his upper body."

Dewey agrees that the man's legs do look underdeveloped in comparison. His hips are slender, but his upper body is massive, with slabbed abs and mammoth biceps.

They jump back, startled, and embrace. He is thawing. His expression relaxes into contentment. The blue cast of his skin fades. His skin is milky, his thighs creamy white. "How come he's not tan?" Dewey asks.

Eddie ignores him. "Come on. He needs our body heat."

Dewey rolls his eyes. "Aren't you suddenly the practical one." But he doesn't argue.

They strip and climb onto the bed, one on either side of him, pressed up tight. They spear his thighs with their aroused worship. Against their sun-dark bodies, his skin is snow, white-white from top to bottom, no tan lines. His long hair dries into wiry curls, resembling his thatch of sea-weedy pubic hair and full beard. His black eyelashes lie dark and long against his alabaster cheeks. Like a wax figure, the rest of his body is smooth.

They roll him onto his side. Eddie is immediately at his tits, gulping them in. He drinks nectar, mead, the golden waterfalls of Olympus. His body crooks around the thrust of that godly cock.

In back, without thinking, Dewey cups the titan's marble cheek. His hand is a magnet compelled by an exotic force. Normally hyper-cautious, he doesn't pause to consider protection. He maneuvers his cock, then yelps. He has plunged his dick into a bucket of ice water. And something else. He glimpses centuries of stored-up pleasure. But he's gone soft from the frigid shock. He cannot penetrate this glacial soul. He whimpers a small noise of frustration.

Eddie releases the man's breast, feeling drugged. He is surprised at the boldness of his lover, the wallflower he has to peel onto the dance floor and into backrooms. His eyes meet Dewey's over the man's shoulder. The morality of what they are doing is slippery. This could be called a dirty word, a crime. But something drives them, pounding at them with the insistence of centaur hooves, the primal beating of drums. They know the man wants it, even in his unconsciousness. He emits a beckoning aura, pulsing. He sweeps across their senses, a lighthouse beacon, leaving them intermittently blinded. He lures them even in glassy stillness.

"Let me." They switch places, climbing over the bewitching body, caressing each other as they pass. Eddie aims his cock into this live flotsam, grimacing as frozen tongues lap at his dick. As slick inside as it is outside, the body closes around him. Eddie bucks, frantic—it will freeze shut, lock his cock in its shark jaws, abutting icebergs grinding him into pulp.

But then Eddie moans. He's never felt anything like this, though he's slept with half the nearest continent. This cavity undulates, murmurs, ripples with waves of seaweed in a current. A swarm of jellyfish pulses, gelatinous, against him. Silken eels weave melodies around his cock. Eddie rides a seahorse through a watery realm. He digs in with his heels, bruising ivory flesh.

In front, the noises of his partner warm Dewey's arousal. He takes that supernatural cock into his mouth whole. The slippery cock creeps down his throat, leaking sea foam and whitecaps. It thrums and hums inside him. Dewey takes in the trident of cock and balls. Color shoots behind his eyes. He drifts in an underwater cavern. Vivid-hued coral dissolves in his mouth. He buries his nose in seaweed. He pumps through the ocean depths, swimming down, the cock is down, farther down his throat, in his lungs, in his intestines, breaching his asshole from the inside out. Dewey swallows the tides. He feeds on godly ambrosia. He nurses octopus ink. It stains his insides, so that every nerve and synapse and bone and shred of tissue glows through his skin. He will light up from the inside and explode.

The lovers both explode, simultaneously. They swim in their own slippery juices.

The titan's body relaxes. He is pliant. He fits into Eddie's curve behind him. His plywood-plank resistance eases. His body's frozen clutch thaws, releases Eddie's cock from inside him. Dewey eases his mouth off that divine cock, gulps in air.

This singular part of him, a Corinthian column—its base nestled in curlicues of wiry hair—remains an ice statue, stubborn in its thrust. The man makes a gurgling noise of agitation. He presses back against the one, presses forward against the other, an undulating fish movement on the bed, a flap of demand and desire.

The lovers need him again. They can't explain themselves, can't rationalize their actions. They can only obey a siren call that beats at them with the insistence of whales slamming their bodies against the ocean surface. They surge with a tide. They are caught in a flood. They have rammed up against the dam of this creature's body. They don't yet know whether this temptation will be their salvation or destruction.

They trade places. Dewey, now behind the man, opens him, eases in cautiously, remembering the biting frost of that ass. No frigid jolt this time, only water lilies blooming across his buried cock. Phosphorescent plankton tortures him with invisible, whispered caresses. Bubbles burble secrets along his shaft. Passing phantasmal fish torment him with transparent fins. Dewey gasps, takes in a mouthful of the man's kelp-forest hair, and moans. He rolls onto his back, pulling this sleeping lover on top of him, still embedded in this dreamscape grotto.

Eddie props the joined pair up against pillows, so they are half-reclined, both facing him, though Dewey is mostly hidden behind the big man. Eddie straddles them, legs stretched wide, and lowers himself onto the sovereign cock that coaxes, commands, compels. He is frightened. He understands this union will bless him with pain. It is a pillar that holds up the roof of the world. He cannot possibly encompass it. But he cannot resist its pull. It guides his open body, harpoons him, and climbs up inside him. Once connected, Eddie cannot pull back. The man's pubic hair en-tentacles him, and he must sink down, down. Eddie yells, his arms spread wide. The cock is a steel rod through his body, holding him up straight. He is a trembling building in an earthquake, and this cock girds him up.

And the man is moving now, though not awake. He is a swimming fish, his body fluid movement as he pushes through water. A continual reversing "S," he swims through them, steers them. They cling to him, one cleaving him, one cleaved by him. He is so far inside Eddie's body on top of him that his cock is Eddie's tongue. His hips are forward, now back. Each pulse of his body shoots pleasure through all three. They surf cresting tidal waves. They invade Atlantis. The pair grips his hair to remain astride. They penetrate icebergs, the Great Barrier Reef, the earth's core. They drink hot lava at the base of submerged volcanoes.

His cavernous yell roars out of him like the frothing sea. He bucks and fills the body of the one on top of him, a raging river that

17

breaks its banks. His icy sap flows and flows until Eddie thinks he will drown from the inside out. A vast ice floe melts inside him. Eddie's back goes numb from the cold oozing through him. He is saturated. Paralyzed. He'll crack into pieces in a breath of arctic wind.

The drowned man's eyes flutter open. They are ocean-depth blue. His square fist comes up. It will connect with Eddie's jaw. But as a drowning man reaches for a driftwood log, it instead closes on Eddie's swollen cock thrust toward his face.

His grip is hard, but his palm is bath water soft. He squeezes, but keeps his hand still, as if he will wring the life juices out of the one whose body he still possesses, his cock still solid and expansive within the rider on top of him, though he has come in torrents. Eddie bounces in his hand, mad for relief. He swirls inside a whirlpool, banging against its sides, desperate for release. He struggles to swim upward, toward air, but he is caught in a riptide that pushes him under. He can't escape this anchored cock. It has grown within him, pierced his innards.

Eddie shouts, bucks, and that cock still buried deep inside him, still spilling a waterfall, still an unthawed icicle, hard and cold, seems to emerge from his throat. It splays his body wide open. He is impaled upon this Greek column that holds up temples, too much for a mortal man.

Eddie sprays the face of the drowned man. He shudders. He would fall over if the man didn't buoy him up, the cock inside him forging a new spine, Eddie's shrinking cock still locked in his grip.

The man licks the life-creating substance, tastes it, touches his free hand to it and rubs his fingers together. He holds his fingers to Eddie's mouth, feeds him a taste of himself. He grabs the back of Eddie's neck, brings him down into a kiss. Eddie drinks in the salt water that covers planet Earth. The titan's beard tendrils hiss and tangle in Eddie's hair, binding him close. The man's tongue flickers deep, touches the tip of his own cock inside Eddie's guts.

Dewey, still lodged behind them, hears the titan's thunderbolt shout, hears Eddie's mortal echo a minute later, feels the vibration of their seismic heaving, cries out with the pulsing grip of the body he trespasses into. Juices flow out of his lover's body onto his legs, onto the bed, flooding the cabin floor. Dewey cannot move, his body pinned by the stab of his own cock in that holy passageway. He is one of those tiny creatures attached to the body of a whale.

Dewey flails, drowning, trapped in a swirling eddy. He reaches around, grabs those two inky nipples.

The frozen man gasps and murmurs. He throws the one on top of him off. Eddie lands with a splash and a yelp on the floor, his body a gaping hole, still trickling brine.

The titan rolls off the one behind him. Dewey cries out. His cock thrusts, seeking connection.

The man turns over, takes Dewey's suddenly abandoned cock into his mouth. He swallows it, ingests it, digests it. He eats in the nuts, chews on them. His tongue reaches back to the asshole, violates the barren tunnel of this body's exit. The tentacled tongue snakes through the mortal passageways, explores its inner fjords down to the fingertips, laps at the inner ear and tickles the scalp insides, flicks at the inner nipples.

Dewey thrashes. The frozen man feeds him his fist, corks his cries. The stuffed man suckles.

The titan retracts his tongue. He stuffs his fist up the asshole, instead. He stuffs his other hand down that mortal throat until his paired knuckles touch under the navel, tectonic plates shifting under tender skin. Dewey's cock is still down his throat. His tongue parts the cock slit, creeps inside, penetrating its length. He will swallow the entire man gulp by gulp.

Eddie scrambles behind him, sneaks his puny cock inside that infinite cave. He is a tiny pearl locked in an immense oyster. He clings tight. The trio bathes at the base of rainbows, circles the equator, tours ice castles. The man shoots liquid silver in their wake.

~ * ~ * ~

The man motions to the light of sunrise pouring in through the hold. He half walks, and the lovers half carry him up to the deck, splashing through the knee-deep, iridescent water, the flood of his eternal arousal. Each step seems to cause him pain. They, too, walk gingerly. They are raw and chafed to their cores. He has possessed and baptized every bodily crevice. They are disintegrating shrapnel in the wake of his unquenchable lust. His cock still rises, threatens. They are wary of it, crave it. They quiver like jellyfish, exhausted. He has wrung them out like sponges, milked them dry. They are empty of human fluid. They are cleansed and purified. He has filled them with his own piscine juices.

He blinks into the sunrise, inhales, tosses his hair in the crisp breeze. In the rising wind, the rigging smacks the spars with a discordant *ping, ping*. The boat keels and turns, as though skirting the rim of a vortex. He stretches and rubs his chest. He looks up at the ship's sky-reaching mast, touches his own, clamps it in the jaws of his fist, and roars. He fills the ocean with his salt spray. On their knees beside him, the lovers paw at his clenching haunches. They are two babbling brooks.

He dives overboard with a quiet splash, his body parting the water, legs transforming into scales and flukes before he disappears beneath the sea. He bobs up close to the boat and beckons.

The lovers look at each other, deciding. They touch hands.

He impatiently slaps his green tail on the surface of the water.

His lovers slip in after him into the frigid depths, their new tails unfurling and glistening under the red sky.

Vamp

I know you'll think this is all *ho'omalimali*, but I swear I'm not bullshitting you.

He pressed one hand into the back of my knee before I knew he was behind me. I was up on my tiptoes on the University of Hawaii Library footstool, reaching for *Haunted Hawaii* on the top shelf, looking for material to spice up my tour guide rap. His cold hand startled me, and I lost my balance. His other hand slid up the back of my cutoffs. He cupped my *okole*, the left cheek, and pushed me back upright. I'm sure he was expecting underwear, but once I strip off my bright flowered work uniform, *pau hana*, I wear as little as possible and I was going commando.

He didn't take his hands away. He owned me with his touch. He could crumple me down or hold me up, however he pleased.

I didn't know who he was, where he came from, or how long he'd been watching me.

His hand slipped down from my *okole* and crept into the tight cranny between my thighs, searching for my balls, but they were sweaty and squashed tight up under the denim inseam. My big

22

legs make for a tight fit, and he gave up trying to extricate my *ohana* jewels. He ran his hands up and down my legs. I stared at those disembodied hands exploring my body, his skin on mine like white coconut meat against its tough brown husk. Even his long fingers couldn't make it all the way around my mountain-biking calves. He touched me like he couldn't believe I was real. I didn't turn around to face him. I didn't want to snap out of a surreal dream. Maybe this was Maui the Trickster playing a godly joke on me.

He had his nose right at my tailbone. He pulled my sleeveless tank out of my waistband. He ran his hands under my shirt, across my back, and around to my abs. My nipples were on high beam, what with his icy touch and the air-conditioning cooling my sweat. It didn't take long for his Braille exploration to find them, plus I've got big tits. He reached up and pinched them hard. He touched both hands to my throat.

He dipped his fingertips down my belly and into my waistband. He paused as he encountered the tip of my *ule*—like a second glance, but instead of sight, touch—surprised by its half-mast reach. No bragging, I'm a big dude, and my cock's proportionate. He popped open my fly. My shorts dropped easily to my ankles once he got them over my ass mounds—they're the size of the outer islands.

I had those sweet thong tan lines that come spreading out from your ass crack like embracing wings that reach around to cup your precious jewels. I could've sunbathed nude on my apartment's dinky lanai, but I think those tiny lines look really hot on muscular bodies like mine. They make big asses look penetrable. Front and back, those lines draw the eye right to the point. That's one part of me I don't care to sunburn, plus I'm *hapa*, mixed race, and I like to think I've stuffed my white side right up my ass.

He pressed his lips, cold and dry and thin, right to my crack. I must have been real *hauna*, but he seemed to like that musky smell. He breathed me in and licked my salty skin. Fresh from a hard bike ride through the Manoa Valley, I'd hit the library more for the cold air than the books. My studio apartment's air-conditioning was busted, but they kept the library A/C cranked because mildew is such a problem on the collections, what with the humid climate.

His white hands snaked through my pubic hair, the same coarse dark curls as the ones on my head. He cupped my package, feeling its heft. My *ule* protested his freezing hands. I mean, I was naked in the library, for crying out loud. I've had some kicks before, but never anything like that. He laughed when I wilted. But with what his cold fist did to my uncertain *ule*, I was stiff as a surfboard in seconds.

He worked me over *wiki wiki*. I thought he rushed because he was afraid of getting caught. Later I realized he wanted to show me good and fast that I had absolutely nothing to do with it. All I could do was give up and follow his paces. He revved me up before I could really go, like peeling tires when you take off too fast. He laid a patch with my body, and afterward I felt like one of those retreads you see at the side of the road. I didn't have time to think about any of it. I gave up to him, just like that, pawing a little at the stool with my toes. His moving hand was a blur, like a white dove flapping her wings. I smelled the burning sugar cane fields of my childhood, when the ash would drift over the schoolyard.

He bit my *okole*, and I erupted all over the book spines. So much for mildew. I lost all strength to my legs. Weak-kneed, I sagged back against him, and he lifted me down. Yeah, lifted, like in the *Gone with the Wind* poster, me looking up at him in a faintish, goofy sort of way. Nobody's hefted my sizable carcass since I was a little *keiki*. I'm big. And I don't act queeny or vamp it up, so I don't look *mahu*. How did he know he wasn't going to get a fist in his face instead of my sweet *okole*? His confidence and assumption were what really grabbed my attention—well, that and what he did to me in the stacks, only I guess he grabbed more than that.

His power and my unresisting surrender went straight to my groin, and I went stiff again. My thick *ule* has this way of looking purple and angry and demanding when it's awake. It's a mean cock. It surprises people if they know me. The head roars, like you'd better think twice about letting it down, and right now it was pointing straight at him in stubborn command. He liked the Second Coming. I could tell by his smile. Plus, it was his first good look; he'd had his face full of my twin volcanoes up till now.

He set my naked butt on the stool. It had one of those ribbed, non-skid rubber coverings, and it dug graph-paper lines into my *okole*, smarting where he'd given me the ass hickey. Only now my cock pointed straight up at me, like to say, "You big dummy. Neener neener."

"Just let me go wash my hands," he whispered, with a librarian gesture of finger to lips, flashing his rings. "I'll be right back."

I sat there 38 minutes, waiting. I should've expected as much from a blonde; they act so entitled. The librarian kicked me out after the third closing announcement. I almost asked her if she wanted to play tic-tac-toe on my ass, but I'd hiked up my shorts by then. I left the books all *kapakahi* where I'd almost pulled them down on myself while he milked my *poi*-pounder.

That's how it started.

I should have considered it a one-night stand. Why else would he ditch me naked on a library stool? But I knew he had something else in mind. He had purchased me from the shelves with those hands. He had marked me like a due date stamp. I had to sit with my right ass cheek cocked up off the seat for a week because of my bruised *okole*, had to sleep on my *opu* because sleeping on my back aggravated the sore spot. There had to be something in it for him. I mean, I hadn't even touched him.

I prowled the stacks every night after dumping off busloads of sunburned tourists at their Waikiki hotels. How else was he going to find me? I even tried to jerk off standing there, but the librarian cruised by, so I packed myself away real quick.

Eventually I gave up and rode my bike to the other side of the island and up the trail to Sacred Falls. It was late by the time I got there, and no one was around, so I stripped. I climbed the rock cliff and dove into the freezing pool. The water was his body and breath against me. His icy touch, and his gaze, gripped and penetrated me. I frog-kicked across the pool, and the water fucked my ass crack.

I paddled my outrigger furiously under the water, needing the friction to heat my *ule*. I'd been sticking my hand in the freezer before masturbating—which was constantly—remembering his cold strokes. My waves splashed the surface as much as the waterfall.

I swam under the pounding falls. The avalanche of water beat at my body and suffocated me. I latched onto the rock ledge and splayed my legs. The cascading water slammed into my ass, making violent, fluid love to me. It pushed me down into the depths of the pool, drowning me as it fucked me.

I floated back to the surface in still water downstream, my cock bobbing up first like a shark fin. I hummed the *Jaws* theme. The cold water lost its grip, and the warm air caressed me. The mist from the falls was all I'd need to come, I was that close. But I splashed upright, taking in a lungful of water. My bike and shorts were gone from the rock bank. Not only had someone stolen my stuff, but they'd witnessed my little water ballet. And now I had to find my way back in the dark without my bike light. Naked.

I ran. My hungry cock led the way awhile, until it got smacked a couple of times by stray branches. The dense mountain foliage scratched me, and I tumbled over exposed roots. My callused *luau* feet could take the rocks; hell, I could walk on hot pavement and broken glass. It was the fear of *menehunes* that bothered me. The evil Hawaiian version of leprechauns, they lurked at night, ready to attack. These creatures had haunted me since my old Tutu, who had raised me, told me ghost stories when I was a *keiki*. I hadn't outgrown the superstition. I had no idea how I was going to get home halfway around the island once I escaped the forest. I just knew I had to *hele* on out of those deserted woods before something grabbed me.

I staggered, naked, dirty, bruised, and scratched, into the dark parking lot. My bike was strapped to the trunk of his Porsche convertible. He didn't speak or wave, just watched.

Pissed, I strode over to him. Anger brings out my local features in hard lines, and I knew I looked mean. Only, my *tiki* torch lit up…I was that charged by his reappearance, so I guess I wasn't all that threatening. He just smiled.

I like his smile.

There was no sign of my shorts.

I climbed into the passenger seat and fastened my seat belt. He wasn't wearing his. He touched my thigh, and I got chicken skin. He fingered a welt on my shaft. He shifted my gears and the car's as he drove through the night. Without headlights. *Pupule*, man. Crazy. He took me to Paradise Park, which was closed for the night. The exotic birds squawked in their tourist trap, like groups of lady tourists do when I step off the bus; they all chitter and chirp, pointing at me, especially if I bend over to tie my shoe. It makes a difference in tips, God love 'em.

"Ever been inside?" he asked me.

"Not since elementary school." I told him how I'd gone home crying over the caged birds, had drawn up daring plans to free the parrots.

I followed him to the entrance. He had my clothes. He jimmied the locked front gate.

The giant birdcage is two stories tall, and you enter at the top. We stood at the beginning of the descending path that zigzags down around one side of the open-barred cage. The tropical birds, their blaze of colors refracted in the dim pathway lights, flapped their wings and shrieked at the late-night disturbance. I started to walk down the path, but he grabbed my hand. I jumped with its chill.

I kept walking. Now that his hand wasn't on my cock, I was mad again.

I couldn't pull free. He stood still and quiet, just holding me. I whiplashed back.

I liked the shock of it. I had really checked him out this time, and he looked too thin to push me around. He's almost as tall as me, and older, with washed-out blue eyes and blonde hair slicked back, like one of those proper dudes on a boring public television movie about a different century. He wore light-colored linen clothes that whispered around his body in the trade wind. His style is expensive but simple, except he wears a few big-ass rings, like even on his thumbs, thick and gold and hammered. One caught on my cock head in the stacks, and later he liked to scratch me with the diamond one.

He's *haole*, real white. Like, white in a way even *haole*s in Hawaii just aren't. Walking between your car and the minimart will give you color. I mean, how could you stay that white with a convertible in the tropics?

He stuffed my clothes into the cage, shoes and all. They fell to the bottom, two stories down. Had to be bird shit down there.

He grabbed my cock and led me down the path to the cage door at the bottom. He held it open for me. I stepped in, and the barred door slammed behind me with a clang. I tested it. Locked from both sides. I'd worry about that later. Right now he beckoned to me through the bars. I came up close, and he petted me. I thought I'd shoot instantly. I'd never been put in a cage before. But he wasn't about to allow what he'd given me so quickly in the library. He'd just started to play. Tonight wasn't about my coming *wiki wiki* again. It was about stretching out my torment.

He rattled a pocket full of change. The birds squawked for a midnight snack, expecting us to feed them treats out of the vending machines. He bought a pile of seeds for them, stuffing his pockets, and scattered them at my feet. They swooped down, screeching. The beaks and claws on those birds made me real nervous.

I stood with my back to him, my *okole* pressed against the bars. He reached into the cage to fondle me, the other hand alongside my *ule*, with a handful of seeds. I wanted my dick to shrink down out of the birds' way, but he made sure it stood up for them. They flapped around me, screeching and pecking. He balanced a seed right on my cock head, and a nasty white parrot swooped in and pecked it off. I yelped and slammed back against the bars. He laughed.

I like his laugh.

I felt a nagging tickle up my ass. He'd fitted me with a plumed tail. It wagged whenever I clenched my cheeks.

He allowed me to turn around, cock thrust out of the cage and swollen balls hooked up over a crossbar. He walked a few more steps up the path and extended his enticing fingers into the cage. Up I climbed while he strummed my *ukulele*, my "jumping flea," until he stood at the top again. Two stories up, I clung to the cold bars, slippery with my sweat, my cock demanding a feeding through the cage. The height didn't bother me. I'd climbed a lot higher up mountainous rock that hadn't offered such easy hand- and footholds. But the parrots worried me. They screamed and beat with their wings, suspicious of this tailed beast in their sanctuary. He encouraged their raucous dance around me, sprinkling seeds on my hair and shoulders, on my ass hills, and wedged in my ass crack above my tail.

I wanted to climb down a few notches and have him feed me his shaft. Polly wanted some *kau kau*. I wanted him to pound down into me, his passion threatening to dislodge me, the danger of a high-rise blow job heightening my lust. But he just kept petting me, a slow, persistent stroke. He plucked one of my tail feathers and dusted my *ule* with it. That's how slow he went. He had me clinging to that cage, squawking as loud as the parrots.

I trembled from the strain of holding my weight up for so long. I started to climb down. But he took such a hold of my dick it seemed he'd rip it out by the root if I moved, so I stayed planted, him working me over, my tail drooping.

He picked up the pace, and Polly sang.

He made me turn around, a dangerous execution, my back to the cage as I clung to it, arms above me, heels tucked into an

31

opening. He reached around to my cock. I rocked in his motionless fist, the dance up to me. The bars rattled as my ass beat back against them, crushing my tail. He crouched and bit my ass again. I yelped, almost losing my hold, but instead shot an impressive arc that fell like warm tropical rain. I lost my tail.

I turned around. I should have guessed. He was gone. Only this time he'd left me in a trickier spot than bare-assed on a library stool.

Muscles quivering with exhaustion, I climbed down, slipping off my foothold a couple of times and dangling dangerously. I pulled on my cutoffs, swearing as the white parrot crapped on my head. I'm not sure what made me look up, but there he stood at the top, expressionless, next to an unlatched cage door. I had to climb back up to get out.

Flopping through the door awhile later, seal-like, I heard him screech out of the parking lot. He left me a present with my bike: the most brilliant multihued feather I'd ever set eyes on. I'd heard a hell of a shriek and suspected it was fresh plucked.

I could hardly make it home. With twin hickeys on my ass cheeks, one fading and one fresh, I coasted into the sunrise, standing up on the pedals.

After that I masturbated with the feather instead of ice cubes.

~ * ~ * ~

He stopped making me wait so long between visits. He showed up without warning, always at night. Whenever he appeared, I *hele*'d on over as fast as I could, no matter where I was. I'd ditch my friends. Takeout from Zippy's Drive-In couldn't compare to his *pupu* platter. After a while my buddies gave up on me and quit calling.

He drove me all over, often to the same places I took jackass happy tourists during the day. While the pink herds milled around outside snapping photos, I jerked off on the tour bus, remembering what he'd done to me on this very spot, hours before. I was marking his territory—namely, me. I preferred his package tours to mine. Despite the daytime crowds, the places were deserted at night. One look from him, his narrow nose flaring, and any strays scampered. He wasn't physically threatening, like I could be. There was just something about him, a powerful *mana*. Like *auwe*, dude, if you crossed him wrong. I did my share of scampering.

Our dates consisted of one thing: me naked and him touching me, watching me. No small talk.

He'd tease and torture me all night. When I staggered into work the next morning, my boss thought I was stoned on *pakalolo*. I started calling in sick. I was afraid I'd wreck the tour bus, shouting "*Alo-o-o-HA!*" as I rid the island of myself and a gaggle of tourists. I went surfing. The ocean purified me, his scratches stinging in the saltwater.

By the time he took me up to the old *heiau* above Waimea Bay, I was cranky. I was getting tired of this routine. All he did was push me around and watch me squirm. I had yet to touch him. He hadn't removed a scrap of clothing. He hadn't even kissed me. He paid my dick lots of attention, but that's it. I reached for his crotch in the car. He smacked my hand away, and I sulked. I thought about dumping him, moving on and finding a real relationship.

I knew I couldn't. There were worse things than a guy paying too much attention to your dick. But the thought made me feel like I had a choice.

The *heiau*'s not much more now than a low, crumbling rectangular wall of rocks overgrown with weeds. Wandering around the sacred temple of the ancient Hawaiian *kahuna* witch doctors creeped me out. Humans had been sacrificed to the gods here, but he prowled around like he owned it, no fear. At least at night we didn't have to worry about throwing our shadows across the *kapu* rocks. The taboo would have brought a death curse down upon us, or so the old people believed. I wrapped a smooth *ti* leaf around one of the small rocks and set it down amidst similar offerings left by others. Some *haole* brainiac had supposedly disproved that the ancients ever did that, but plenty enough still believed.

"For good luck," I explained sheepishly.

"Amazing the power the dead have over us, isn't it?" he asked. I felt pretty stupid.

He couldn't get me off, though on the way over my cock had been raging. I was too intimidated by my childhood superstitions, and he seemed to like that even better than my unfailing hard-ons. He smacked my soft meat around a little bit, and I asked again if we could go someplace else.

34

He pushed me facedown, naked of course, across the *kapu* rocks I'd always avoided even with my shadow. He finger-fucked me, his first penetration of my body. I bucked at the shock, mostly because I hadn't expected it after all this time, and his finger was dry and cold. I wanted up but couldn't push him off. I struggled a moment, then gave up to him. I couldn't refuse him. He explored my insides a long time, brutally, adding fingers. I tried to crawl away, but he was leashed to my insides. He pulled me back, scraping my torso and cock on the volcanic shrapnel. I knew he wouldn't stop until I broke down and accepted that my body must obey him. I tried to relax and open myself to the penetration I'd been craving.

He rolled me over. My body rotated around his fist like a *huli huli* chicken. He licked at my stinging scrapes. I was still limp, playing slack key. He spread my legs, made me hike my ass up. He pulled his hand out and shoved my slick *ti*-leaf-wrapped sacred rock right up my shameless *okole*.

"Dance," he said.

I don't know how he knew about my *hula*. I never talked about it. It was sacred, pure, the best part of me. I had refused to earn better money at it by entertaining the tourists.

"Why do you do this?" I rarely asked questions. When I did, he rarely answered.

"Because I'm bored."

Beats television.

I knew he wouldn't ask twice. If I said no, I'd never see him again.

I rose up on my knees and chanted in the ancient language. I knew better than to drop the rock.

Real hula isn't smiling girls in grass skirts shaking their skinny *okole*s for the tourists. Nobody danced that crap till the *haole*s came. Ancient hula used to be a preparation for war, serious business, men only. The *kane*s stomp and chant *mele*, telling a story with their hands. It's real macho, but graceful and beautiful.

I danced on my knees, *noho*, in the dirt and weeds inside the decomposing wall, the soil rich with ancient blood. I danced and danced, but I couldn't get it up. I knew I couldn't stop dancing until I'd proven that he ruled my body. He'd fitted me with the proverbial red shoes, only they were up my ass, and I was dancing where the spirits could kill me.

So instead of the rain and sea and volcanoes and ancient gods, I made up a chant, a dance, about him. He possessed and penetrated me, even when he wasn't near. I beseeched him, paid homage to him, offered myself as sacrifice for his pleasure. He filled my mind and body, invading every crevice. He could kill me with his curse, or rule me with his mercy.

My cock obeyed, growing as hard as the rock inside me. I felt huge and primeval, like the petroglyph stick figures the ancients carved in rock, their phalluses monstrous and out of proportion.

I stood up and danced faster, building a crescendo with the *kaholo*, the "vamp" step. My muscles quivered with the struggle of holding the rock inside me. I collapsed to my knees, but I didn't lose it.

"Set it down there." He pointed to the most hallowed rock, a flat stone where I'd always imagined the victims had been killed. The rock, like the dirt around it, had a reddish hue. As with everything he commanded, I obeyed and crawled over to him.

He'd broken me. He had tested me and discovered no limits. He was God over me, *akua* and *aumakua*, greater and lesser, *kahuna* and *ali'i*. His worship left room for no others.

He didn't touch me.

I could've used a hug.

He took me up to Waimea Falls, and I dove off the high cliff into the deep pool of water. I felt cleansed and let him fondle me when I climbed out. I wanted to come, desperately, a release for my conflicted emotions. But he wouldn't take me there. It pissed me off. The turmoil had exhausted me, and I reached down to finish myself off. He grabbed my wrist, but I was so close and the struggle such a turn-on, I knew I would come without direct contact. He threw me into the cold water. My cock retracted like a frightened snake.

He wound me up again on the ride home, then dumped me out of the car in front of my crummy apartment, right on the brink.

He had never deprived me of satisfaction before. I guess I expected a tip for my performance.

That's when he told me I couldn't come anymore when he wasn't around. No more rubbing it out.

Yeah, right. Good luck with that, *haole*.

Except I couldn't. Much as I tried, much as it hurt not to take it that last stroke over the edge, I couldn't. I walked around with a raging boner and could hardly take a piss in the morning, I was so stiff.

He waited a long time before turning up again.

When I next saw his blinking headlights, I trotted over, deserting the *luau* dinner package tour. He saw I'd obeyed. My barometer wouldn't lie. I bulged right out of my pineapple-print *malo*, and the loincloth's wedgie wasn't helping matters any. I couldn't keep the front flap down, and the ladies were tipping better than ever. He reached over the car door and ripped it off, leaving it in a heap on the pavement. Tourist jaws dropped wider than the *kalua* pig's. I climbed in. He backed over my outfit before peeling away.

His hands gripped the steering wheel. I wished they'd grip something else. I ached. I needed him. Now. I didn't care about reality tomorrow.

He took me to his place for the first time. He has this massive house right on the water, with automatic gates and everything.

"You live here alone?"

"I keep a few houseguests."

I laid back on a scarlet couch, the type where fainting ladies in corsets stretch out. The chandelier over us actually had candles.

He kissed me. That was a first. I drank it up like crazy. I tried to rub against him, but he pulled away.

"Live with me," he said. "Be mine."

"Okay."

A hell of a deal. So what if he couldn't get it up? Since I'd seen no action behind the fly of his tailored slacks, I'd guessed that impotence forced him to get his kicks through other displays of power. I could live with that.

He flipped me over and poured a bottle of celebration champagne up my ass. I'm telling you, this stuff was no Riunite. The liquid bubbles made me squirm and laugh, and he fucked me with the bottle. It was a hell of a lot better than the rock. I erupted just like the uncorked bottle. He didn't worry about ruining the velvet settee.

My groom led me—by my hand—to my suite of rooms. Yeah, suite. He had totally decked out my bedroom for a real wedding night, everything in white, and candles and gardenias all over—he knew I'd say yes. A filmy canopy floated over the bed. We'd never done it in a bed before.

He shoved me facedown on the mattress, just dug right into my neck with his shark's teeth. He'd always nibbled at me, licking at my scratches, but nothing could have prepared me for this rabid penetration of my flesh in his intense lust and hunger. I went rigid, like in a paroxysm.

I wasn't surprised once it happened.

And I wasn't afraid.

His cock bulged against my backside as he grew hard on my blood. I pressed back, wanting it in an unbelievable way. He was warm against me. I had my mouth open in one long, nonstop moan. Despite my sudden anemia, I stayed pumped up and wanting it, his expert hand reaching around to fondle me.

39

He wanted a lover, not a victim, *maké*, a corpse. I guess quickies had lost their flavor for him decades or centuries ago, just like they do for most of us. He wanted me to want it, passion returned in his all-consuming embrace. I would hunger for it like he hungered for me. I was addicted, infected, incurably diseased.

I knew what I was going to be.

It's not so different from what his type's been doing to our people for centuries.

Maybe you think I'm *lolo*, crazy, but what kind of future was I giving up? The land has been stripped and paved. No sugarcane now, either. Everything's endangered, even water. What's left? I'd been serving *haole*s my ass on a plate all along, only I preferred the way he fed off me.

He turned me over so I could watch him. He undressed. There was nothing wrong with his anatomy as far as I could see, his white shaft swollen and tinged with my own blood coursing through his ancient veins.

He fucked me, missionary-style, just like the first religious invaders to the islands taught us. I gave myself to him. I am his. My body is *kapu* to all others now, off-limits, sacred, property of my king and god, *ali'i* and *akua*. He rammed hard and deep and cold, ruthless, his dick inside me, and latched on again with his mouth to my neck. It was like his two body parts, his dick and lips, connected somewhere deep inside me, like I could feel his dick straight through my body from my asshole up to the top of my spine. I went limp, and it was like an orgasm all through my body, like jamming my finger into an electric socket.

I bucked and gasped, body spasming, brain and body screaming, him half full and me half empty, helpless to anything he desired.

He knew my pace, my rhythm, when he could push me and when I couldn't take any more torment. All this time he'd been testing, training, wooing, punishing, and rewarding me, simultaneously. Because he had to time it just right, leaving me enough to stay hard while taking enough to pump up his lust and fuck me. He liked to make it last, but he didn't want to kill me.

He couldn't climax. The pleasure he got was the sensation of the fucking, of being alive, of the body beneath him wanting it, of sex linked with live prey.

We are symbiotic, the perfect couple. He needs me, and he's my dream lover. Would you leave a man who fucks you all night long and doesn't care about his own orgasm?

So, you see, no *ho'omalimali*, I live to tell the tale. And I'll go on living. I'm not what you think I am. I'm not like him, not one of his kind. My body replenishes what he needs. I eat lots of steak. Watching me eat turns him on.

Sure, he snacks on the occasional tourist, but their sunscreen nauseates him. I like to think he chooses the ones Darwin would take care of, anyway, like the morons who head out to surf when the *tsunami* sirens wail. Or the ones who, despite all the warning signs, look down into the Blow Hole and get sucked into the lava tube by a big wave before you can say *dumbfuck*. Or the ones. On those nights, he wakes me with his cock in my mouth and he can seem almost content while I suck him off for hours. They say drownings on the island are up.

As I gain in strength, his hunger and lust for me grows. And when I've healed from his lovemaking, he saps my strength again with a passion no human lover can match. But first I dance for him, singing his tale in the oral tradition of the ancients. The customary dog-tooth anklets clatter as I chant, only I know these are no poodle canines. These others were disposable, human sacrifices.

But me, he keeps.

Frigid

The door creaked open. A water-logged gust of wind stirred napkins, cigarette ashes, and out-of-date opera posters sagging off the walls—*Faust* buckled at the knees. The breeze crept across the room, whispering behind the bar to flutter Simon's soiled apron. Like a wave rippling calm seas when a magnificent creature breaks the surface, Simon thought, working the beer tap and blowing the keg. Or, long ago, like Simon's hands through Wray's scythed wheat-field hair, tremors trailing his squat fingers through the stiff yellow shocks.

The sound of rain slapping the pavement fought with the jukebox, which heaved out the opera *Rusalka*. Simon played the mermaid's aria in his most melancholy moods. Surf pounded the nearby seashore, booming thunder.

A man stepped across the threshold, tossing wet hair out of his face. Topher dropped his busboy's tray. Shattered glass slashed an eerie silence into the tavern—Rusalka fell mute, and the closing door choked off the hammering rain and fisted ocean waves.

"We're closed!" Simon yelled at the man, crouching and easily replacing the empty with a full, 160-pound keg in the

Kegerator. "I told you to lock the door," he scowled at Topher. Laugh lines furrowed around his eyes told a different tale from his now rare smile.

"I did! I swear! Maybe the lock's busted, like everything else around here."

The stranger swept off his sunglasses and swept his gaze across the room, a lighthouse beacon that settled on Simon as he stood and stripped off his apron.

Topher reached behind Simon for the broom. "Do you have any idea who that is?" he whispered.

"Don't tell me one of your godawful soap opera actors." This one Simon couldn't peg as the villain or the hero.

"Mega pop star, old guard. Sell one photo of him in a gay bar to the tabloids and you'd pay off what you owe on this place. Maybe then my next paycheck wouldn't bounce."

Simon could believe the stranger was no ordinary nine-to-fiver. He possessed the fuck-you beauty of holocaust fashion models slouched in savage clothing on angular furniture. Tonight's few customers had scampered in like wet mutts, all flapping coats and clacking umbrellas and barking displeasure and doleful eyes, grunting and collapsing in sodden heaps. But this one didn't scurry. It would take more than acid rain to corrode the chiseled alabaster of this face. A fine drizzle would cause lesser mortals to beg to hand him a towel and park him before a fire, knowing he'd give you nothing but muddy boots to clean.

Beguiling. Bewitching. But not gay. And yet…something pulsed across the room between them, a careening butterfly of

44

current. "Sorry, closed!" Simon repeated, dousing the electric snap the stranger flicked at him. He dumped out the beer he'd tried to pour for himself after enduring yet another day, the well-earned drink nothing but sediment and foam. "Time for bed."

The stranger perched his sunglasses on his head.

"Don't blow this, Simon." Glass tinkled as Topher swept and whispered. "Either be nice and make friends with his deep pockets, or..." he nodded at the security surveillance camera. "More compromising the pose, the more it'll fetch."

Sunglasses in the rain at three a.m.—Simon had little patience for such displays of self-importance. He ignored Topher and spoke to the stranger, "Don't stand there dripping unless you want to mop it up."

Topher threw down the broom. "For once why can't you listen? Give me a call when you can pay me in cash." To the stranger, he called out, "Come right on in and dry yourself off. Simon's got nowhere to be, except nowhere, fast. Me, I've got someone waiting. Like Simon said, time for beddie bye." Topher sashayed to the door. Behind the stranger's back, he threw one last glare at Simon and pointed at the camera. "Have fun, you two." The door closed behind him, and the dead bolt groaned into its socket.

The stranger cocked his head, narrowed his eyes, and crossed the room, taking his time. His boots beat a sensuous rhythm on the plank floor, occasionally missing a beat as he hit a sticky spot. His damp, black jeans clung, a greedy second skin. He swung his leg over a barstool in front of Simon, as if climbing on a Harley. He set his sunglasses down—a designer brand that cost more than

45

Simon's entire wardrobe, but cracked and bent. His fingers played the bartop, luring Simon under a spell. No rings. No bracelets. No watch. Nothing to detract from the natural grace of his white hands. His fingers never stopped moving, a waterfall of movement working an invisible piano. Occasional slabs of drop-dead beefcake saw the far side of Simon's bar, but this was no Chippendale cookie— something off kilter in his bolted eyes. A scratch nicked one cheek. Fine trembling ran through his body. The long fringe of his jacket danced.

"Suede in a downpour." Again, Simon popped the fuse that circled a crackling frisson between them. "Not too bright, I'd say." The expensive coat now looked like rotting seaweed, ensnaring the stranger in tangled tassels. A bluish cast hazed his anemic pallor. Probably an addict in need of a fix.

The stranger's gaze strayed between Simon and his own reflection in the backbar mirror, the crowning glory of Simon's bar. He'd spent months stripping and refinishing the arch of carved mermaids. But dust now caked their sunken eyes, caught in the ash of Simon's caldera. The bare-breasted ladies would have sneezed if alive.

Simon blew cigarette smoke out of his nose. "You've got the wrong place, pal. Hooters is the next town over."

Amusement flirted with the stranger's impassive expression, a fleeting glimmer in his glistening sealskin eyes, pupil blending into iris in the dim light of the bar. No. Just the headlights from a passing car playing tricks through the closed blinds. "Not a fake breast man, myself."

What a voice. Like the rain itself had come inside to converse. But flat. Emotionless. Out of tune. "Yeah? Well, I doubt you're in the market for what's on tap here."

"Don't be so sure." The stranger held Simon's eyes. His mouth twitched, as if the arched seabird wings of his upper lip might take flight into a smile, but settled back instead on glassy seas. "For starters, I'd settle for a beer. Make that half a beer since I missed last call?"

Simon leaned on the bar, hands splayed flat, beefy arms locked straight at the elbows. He couldn't judge the stranger's years with that unblemished complexion, like porcelain. "Got I.D.?"

"I haven't been carded in years."

"Yeah, so I hear if I didn't have my head stuck in the sand I'd know who you are, but I stopped paying attention when the Bee Gees fucked up *Sergeant Pepper* with a remake."

"C'mon, you would've been in diapers."

"Kindergarten, but it doesn't take potty training to know not to defile a classic. Figured it was all downhill from there. So excuse me if I treat you the same as everyone else. Not like The Man needs much reason to shut down a place like this. Lots more respectable places would like this property."

"Doesn't look like you'd mind." He ran a finger along the bar edge and held his sooty pinky up, smudged like he'd been marked for prison fingerprinting.

Simon leaned forward. The stranger's scent hit him—briny, like the sea, or tears, or sex. "Don't assume too much about me."

"Likewise. For knowing so little about me, you think you know an awful lot."

"I've seen enough to know that if you're swinging in my direction tonight, it's just a game. And I'm a man who's tired of games."

"I can see that. I like that."

"Slumming stars don't impress me."

"I like that, too. But the truth is, I'm lost. Had to run or lose my scalp. You'd be amazed at the strength of hysterical girls. Saw the, uh, explicit signage out front and figured I'd be safe here. From them, anyway. Glad your door was unlocked. Thanks for inviting me in." Another flicker rippled his bland expression.

So, this striking human flotsam wanted some sport with nobody's prize. Fine. Now that he'd drifted in, Simon suddenly wasn't ready to throw him back out. This beached figurehead would steer Simon through the lonely pre-dawn hours, when the city slept coupled together beneath clean cotton sheets while Simon habitually walked the beach alone, watching for the first glimpse of dolphins leaping to greet the sunrise. Sometimes he thought he saw…but no. It was wishful thinking. Pathetic. Especially from a grown man like him. He was no six-year-old girl in a pink tutu.

Simon would boot him out when he grew bored—but he didn't want the stranger choosing to leave. "So whyn't you call your friends to come save you. Have the president send Air Force One."

"Man like me has no friends. Only people he pays."

"Man like me has no friends either. Only people he can't manage to pay."

"Touché, then. How about that beer?"

Simon reached for a cup, flipping the switch on the water kettle. He turned back to find that the stranger had stolen Simon's cigarette out of the ashtray. A small lock of drying hair glowed red. A barbaric smell clawed the air. "Watch it." Simon licked his finger and thumb and reached across the bar. The stranger didn't flinch with the forward thrust of Simon's burly paw, merely inhaled on the cigarette, his lips where Simon's had just been. "Your hair's on fire."

The stranger exhaled. "So you care?"

"I'd hate to ruin something putting it out." Simon snuffed the burning ember between his damp calluses. A coil of smoke rose in the shape of a question mark.

"What a relief. I was beginning to worry you were falling for me." Restless fingers played the cigarette.

Simon wound a lock of the stranger's hair around his finger. Lamplight played with water droplets caught in its blue-black waves. Damp tangles curled past his shoulders, hung in his face and fell in his eyes. The messy look lent him the vulnerability of a waking child, clashing with his haughty pose. The offer in those eerie eyes was no trick of the light. There he sat, provocative eyes on him, plain Simon. What a switch. Wray had liked to ignore Simon, making eyes at everyone, male and female, provoking Simon to jealous, violent lust so that Simon would love and punish him all in the same act. Always fucking, never lovemaking.

And Simon was sure this stranger wanted the same thing— provoke the beast, leaving himself no choice but to submit. Later the stranger could kid himself that he hadn't wanted it. What else could this enchanting enchanted wanderer see in a crusty old barnacle like himself—brown hair, brown eyes, brown skin, brown life? A walking billboard for rough treatment, he had the physique of a teapot on steroids, a barrel chest mistaken for fat under his flannel shirts. Lovers tapped on it, asked if he was hollow, listened for his heartbeat, ha ha ha. When he used to have lovers, that is. Simon toyed with a silky curl, then gave it a tug.

The stranger hooked his hair behind his ear. Cigarette still between his fingers, he brushed Simon's lingering hand with the tip—a harmless singe, but a deliberate, slicing halt to the charged air that throbbed with the bare touch of callus to hair. "That drink?"

Simon stepped back and poured, then set a steaming mug before the stranger.

The stranger flicked at the paper tag fluttering over the lip of the cup. "Tea? You're shitting me."

"Shut up and drink."

The stranger blew on the hot liquid, eyes lowered, dense lashes feathering pale cheeks. Despite the late hour, he lacked the midnight shadow that bristled Simon's face. He took a cautious sip, then another, then a gulp, tipping his head back, throat exposed and working.

He set the drained cup down, wiping the back of his hand against his mouth, running his knuckles back along the seam of his lips. The heat colored his waxen complexion. Something settled within him, like dying waves, and the trembling stopped. "I've done

PCP. LSD. Ecstasy. But you give me tea." He half sang it, ending with a hum that ran off into nothing, his eyes drowsing.

"A poet." Simon leaned forward on his elbows.

"A hack. Future has-been. Sooner than later."

Simon refilled his mug.

He cupped it with both hands, absorbing its warmth, staring into it. He drummed his fingertips on the side of the cup. "Thank you," he said. His wondrous gratefulness brought an unfathomable sorrow to his indifferent surface that just as quickly washed away. A tectonic plate heaved on the cold ocean floor of Simon's heart.

The stranger let out a breath. "So you've never heard of me."

"Don't take it personally."

"Indigo. I'm called Indigo. My brand name, you could say."

"Oh, yeah, I've heard of that."

"Really?"

"Sure, in my crayon box. Good color for bruises."

Indigo pushed the tea away and slipped off his stool, moving about the room in slow unease, an off-course brook etching Simon's landscape. He touched the colored glass of a hanging lamp, wiping his dusty fingers on his wet pants, and drummed his fingers on the domed glass of the jukebox.

"You select the music?" He flipped through the cards.

"Some." Simon and Topher quarreled over the music selection, and they ended up with Sinatra and *Madame Butterfly* as well as Topher's electronic noise. Customers raved over the eclectic mix that threatened to turn Simon's into a hip place despite what

51

Topher called Simon's best efforts to keep it in the red. Then the machine would quit, and Simon would neglect to call the repairman, though he had a nice ass and despite being straight accepted hand jobs in lieu of cash. Simon didn't have the energy to jerk anyone off, not even himself. He savored the silence left by an ebbing clientele.

In a dull undertow of longing, Simon followed Indigo across the room. Simon couldn't catch his breath. Like the moon's limpid arms pulling the tide over his head, the stranger's draw left him no oxygen, only a transparent thread of light to reach for—and miss.

Indigo turned to him. "Play me your favorite." His cold touch left goosebumps on Simon's arm.

"Doubt it's up your alley."

He moved away, brushing Simon with his fringed sleeve. "Chalk up one more thing you could be wrong about tonight." He stood with his back to the end of the bar, elbows cocked and palms on the bartop, and hoisted himself up onto it with ease. Feet dangling childlike, his heels struck the bar side with arrhythmic agitation.

Simon turned the key and pressed the button. Nothing happened. He gave an expert triple rap on the secret spot, fist slicing the air, jukebox shuddering under his punch. The soprano's yearning aria churned into life, like a strangled sea creature coming up for air.

Indigo lay back on the bar top. He clasped his hands behind his neck and closed his eyes. His hair and fringes spread in a plume around him. Coat falling open, his dusk-smudged nipples cast twin stains beneath his white shirt. The ribbed T gripped his chest, sinking into the depression of his navel, a teasing nest for Simon's tongue. The image sent a jolt to Simon's groin, painful in its unfamiliarity. Since Wray's unexpected death a year ago—his absence such an unexpected relief that guilt tormented Simon— desire turned to bile. He'd learned of the accident reading the newspaper. Of course the family—Wray's wife—wouldn't know to contact him, the monster in Wray's dark closet.

An odd echo chased the soprano as Indigo caught the tune and hummed along in a lower register with the foreign words. His singing seemed unconscious, bubbling out of him without intent. Smooth as octopus ink. Inexplicable, carrying meaning beneath the untranslated words, like whale songs haunted with human emotion beyond language.

Sudden, choked agony cut off the soprano's yearning wail. Indigo opened his eyes. He rolled onto his side and leaned on one elbow, distracting Simon with his cocked, angular hip.

Simon swallowed. "Her name's Rusalka. You probably know her better as the Little Mermaid, pre-Disney. She trades in her tail for human legs—it feels like daggers slicing into her when she walks. Disney rewrote the fairy tale's original tragic ending, where she winds up in eternal purgatory because she dared to be what she wasn't supposed to be." Simon sensed that Indigo needed no explanation. Like the stranger's own voice, meaning trilled beneath her words, a hidden spring with an untraceable source. But Simon kept talking, too fast, filling the silence. "She longs to be human so that she can love, and thus be loved. She has the most beautiful voice in the sea. She sacrifices it to become a girl, to be with the man she loves, and she loses her immortality."

Indigo sat up. He pulled off his boots and socks, tossing them away. A puddle of water and sand leaked out of the upturned leather. He stood up on the bar and glimpsed himself in the mirror. He danced a few steps to silence, watching his reflection. He moved with fluid ease, his body a flowing reed to his internal music. He tugged off his jacket and flung it aside. The wet leather clung to the mirror with a tentacle-sucking thwack. It hung over a corner of the frame, blinding the carved sea creatures. He pulled off his white tank top and dropped it. Hairless like a youth, he glowed with a disturbing bluish sheen to his pale skin, as if, like Rusalka, he had emerged from the frigid depths of underwater gloom to be warmed by his lover's consuming embrace. Dark nipples shadowed his ice surface.

He turned away from himself and paced, bare feet squeaking against the thick laminate of the bar top, and stood at the end of the bar. He perched there, toes over the edge, as if about to execute a dive. Simon moved to stand at his feet, gripping Indigo's ankles under the hem of his jeans. Indigo's fragile bones clenched in his fists flared his desire.

Indigo jumped. He snapped free of Simon's hold. Simon reached up to his waist, catching and setting him down. Indigo rested his palms over Simon's, pressing Simon's warm hands to his cold mannequin flesh. Simon leaned in to kiss him, but Indigo jerked away. Simon spat out a mouthful of hair.

Simon shoved him back against the walk-in refrigerator, knocking his head against the steel door. The dull thud of skull on metal reverberated through the sluggish channels of Simon's heart. The crude-drum sound stirred his primitive blood. The familiar surge of sour pulsing in his veins saddened him. Was his own bitter ditch gouged so deep that he could not change course? He wanted to be aroused by the sun's gentle tickle of light through leaves, flirting with the surface of a lazy brook. Not this again. "That's right. Pretend you've changed your mind. Then lie to yourself later about who asked for it." Simon looked deep into those dull eyes, a stagnant pond. Simon shook him against the door, knee pressed to Indigo's crotch. Nothing stirred under Indigo's jeans, though Simon's own inseam threatened to pop. Understanding dawned. "You can't get it up."

Indigo blinked. "They call me a sex god."

"No pity party here. There's worse things to be called."

"You're wrong. Imagine living up to it. The humiliation of knowing you can't, and having to hide it. At first it was brilliant, so many wanting me. There's nothing, no one, I wouldn't try. I tasted everything, everybody. People called me bi, but really it was just excess. I couldn't say no to anything."

"Beats saying no but meaning yes." That had been Wray.

"But it was like staring into the sun. Too much, too long, you go blind. Can't feel a thing. Numb. Idolized by millions, it's what I gave up. Or what deserted me."

Simon grabbed a fistful of Indigo's hair and gripped his throat, rattled him against the cold metal. "So you think you can use me to help you feel again?" Simon turned him around. Shoved his face in the door, perfect features distorted in the reflection. He pressed himself against Indigo's back, an unmistakable and insistent arousal. "Who do you think you are?"

"I don't know." Indigo ran his hands, braille-like, over his wavering image. "I can't see myself."

"So you choose me to smash the mirror?"

Indigo touched the reflection of Simon's eyes. "You saw me. As soon as I walked through the door. You looked right at me. At me. With you, I wouldn't have to pretend."

Simon caressed the slashed scar on the underside of Indigo's wrist.

"I tried again tonight," Indigo whispered. "I lied earlier. Nobody chased me. I walked into the ocean. Just kept walking. So easy. I drowned, everything went black, but then I wasn't alone. Something sang to me, carried me, saved me. I can't explain it. I woke up on the beach. No idea where I was. Nothing looked familiar. And I saw the lights from your place. That song, it called to me. You played it over and over."

"I'm not out to save anybody." Simon let him go, unable to comprehend such misery when nature had bestowed such rare gifts upon him. What right did this dark prince have to slash away a perfection that few were granted? Simon wanted to comfort him, nourish him, kiss his scars, bang his head against the wall.

Indigo turned to face him. "Neither was Prince Charming. He just wanted a little tail." A small smile at his own joke let Simon see what he could be, sun cracking through clouds.

"You're not my kind."

"The Little Mermaid didn't fall in love with her own kind, either."

"And look what happened to her."

"Depends on which version."

"Why me? You could have anybody."

"They treat me like glass. They worship me. You don't."

"So you want me to break you. A big dick to wake Sleeping Beauty and off you go with all the king's horses and all the king's men—except me you leave behind." Simon stared at his own reflection. Could nobody see him? Why not a lover instead of beast? "You've picked the wrong guy."

"I watched you through the window. You looked so sad."

"You mean mad."

"No, a sad, seal face—whiskers and all. Putting the chairs up on the tables like the dead sat on each one. I must have stood outside for an hour, trying to get the sand out of my hair and find the balls to come in here. If you hadn't closed the blinds, I'd probably still be mooning around outside like a pathetic scene from a bad musical. But I had to see you." Indigo's skin seemed leached of all color, almost transparent. "Why chase everyone away?"

"Once upon a time, a long time ago, I loved the wrong kind. And the ending wasn't happy." Simon recognized his own lie as soon as he spoke. He had never loved Wray. He had always held back, refusing to let himself feel anything but the urge to dominate, because it was safe. Never risking his heart. Maybe if he had, Wray would have chosen him. Maybe he and Indigo weren't so different, after all, numbing themselves against hurt.

"So let's do a remake. Like Disney."

"Right, you give up fame and fortune for true love with me? Because I won't be quiet. Been there, done that."

A disturbance crossed the frozen marble of Indigo's face, a tossed stone warping his reflection in a glacial pool. Indigo's hesitation clunked in Simon's gullet.

"Didn't think so. Come on. You'd better get dressed." Simon picked up Indigo's T-shirt, finding it soaked with blood. He looked for a dent or blood smear on the refrigerator door. Had he knocked Indigo's head that hard? Had Indigo seen that capacity for violence? Is that all he wanted?

No, the shirt had lain in a pool of blood on the floor. "Hold still. You've cut yourself." He knelt and inspected Indigo's foot. A shard from Topher's broken glass had gashed the pad. How could Indigo not have cried out? He hadn't even noticed. Simon picked Indigo up and set him on the bartop, like a dirty child set on a candy counter to get his scraped knee cleaned. Indigo clung to him, arms and legs wrapped around him, locked behind Simon's back. Simon stood rigid in the embrace, relaxed into it, hugged him back, buried his face in that mane of hair, smelling of smoke and seaweed, gripped harder.

"You could have done anything you wanted with me. Still could." Indigo's voice sounded far away, though right next to Simon's ear. "You want to. I felt it. But you didn't. Everybody else takes. They took until I was empty. You could sell me out or ask for money. I see the camera. But I know you won't. I was cold, and you gave me something hot to drink."

"I'm not nice."

"Or so you'd have everyone believe. But that's not what I see."

"What do you see?"

"When you looked at me, I saw myself again."

"But then who sees me?" Simon's voice cracked.

"You. When I look at you. When you decide to let me in."

Simon let him go. He pushed Indigo's hair off his forehead, tucked it behind his ears. He shredded the white undershirt and wrapped the wound. He pulled off his flannel shirt and stuffed Indigo's arms into the sleeves, as if dressing a doll.

Indigo lay his cold palm against the massive cask of Simon's bare chest. "I hoped you had enough room in there to love someone like me. But I was afraid. You know how it hurts when your leg falls asleep and then wakes up?"

Indigo leaned in, his eyes closed, Simon's open. More breath than kiss, as if silk fluttered between their lips, their mouths lingered on the edge of touch. The change from not touching to touching was imperceptible…like the tide coming in, when only a long lapse in time reveals a bare rise in the water. Simon could not say when Indigo parted his lips, asking with his tongue for Simon to part his. He tasted of chamomile and salt. Simon felt no familiar urge to transfer power to himself, no desire to lunge forward, pin down, pound his breaching need into another body, swift relief that swiftly turned to despair after a union that left him drained rather than satiated. He stood pliant beneath Indigo's gentle kiss, a sea plant waving in current. Indigo shifted into a pressing, longing insistence. Simon couldn't breathe, helpless in a whirlpool of neon colors darting behind his now closed eyes. Simon's stubble rasped against Indigo's smooth skin. Indigo pulled away.

Simon steadied himself, his legs turned to jellyfish. Kisses with Wray were crushing, tongue-wrestling affairs, the first assault in a swift domination that Wray could provoke with the finesse of a jabbing welterweight—heady at first, a man drowning beneath your open mouth, and then suffocating in the monotony of absolute power. It's what all of his lovers seemed to want, to lie down beneath the stampede of his ramming bull, their bodies bruised beneath the pounding steam of his furious passion. It's all they seemed to think he was capable of. "Who'd you practice that on?" Simon asked. "Some supermodel waif that'd turn to dust if you blew cake crumbs at her?"

"Just you. You're such a skittish rabbit, I didn't want to frighten you away."

"You? Scare me?" Simon moved to the jukebox and commanded Rusalka to sing. "Me a chickenshit bunny. That's a first."

"I've hung out all my dirty laundry. Now confess your secret. Admit it's true."

Simon rocked the jukebox, but Rusalka refused to sing. His fist elicited only silence. He jabbed at buttons, causing a manic flipping through the CD covers. A familiar blur caught his eye, and he flipped back. Indigo crouched on the cover of one, microphone in hand, eyes closed, mouth open as he sang. Bathed in a blue spotlight, fringes silhouetted, one arm stretched out to a frenzied audience. Thousands of them reached for a piece of him, but he hovered just beyond their possessive touch. Simon reached to stroke the cardboard face, but his hand bumped the domed glass, Indigo trapped like an exotic fish in an aquarium, gasping from the imprisoning depths of immortality. Simon knocked at the machine again, but Indigo, too, had fallen mute.

"I've always thought it was the saddest thing, her having to be silent to find love—she never found it. The man she loved had no idea who she really was." Simon turned to face Indigo. Maybe Wray would have leapt if he had faith that Simon would catch him. Indigo, for whatever strange reason, trusted him and risked the fall. The stranger had much more to lose by admitting his shame than Simon. "It's true. Love at first sight, soon as I saw you. And I tried to kick it out." Just as Simon knew he lied when he professed love for Wray, he grasped the absolute truth of struggling against a terrifying eddy when the stranger stepped through the door. He'd seen the fragile glass behind the stranger's carved crystal exterior, wanted to cradle him, and wanted to crush him for the gash of yearning he slashed open.

Indigo hopped down from the bar, wincing on his sliced foot. His body swam in Simon's oversized shirt. He limped across the room. His wonder at the return of pain played across his face, like sunbeams skidding across water. He stopped close in front of Simon. "You almost did. But I knew I could love the man who built this place, who loved it once."

His jacket, slowly drying on the mirror's edge, let loose its sucking hold and dropped to the floor, leaving a swatch of dusted mermaids blinking into the light.

Indigo leaned into him. "So, what d'you say? Am I that sorry of a catch?"

"I'd say it's time to get you out of those wet jeans. Find out if you've got scales."

Stripping him of the damp denim was like peeling a selky's skin. Simon tugged the stubborn, clinging jeans down. They sucked at his ankles. Simon pulled them free. No scales and no underwear. Indigo's drowsy cock was not a humiliation, but vulnerable—like a wet kitten Simon wished to cuddle and protect.

Indigo looked down at it. "Bit of a cursed frog at the moment."

"A few hundred kisses will lift it."

"You look that up in your fairy godmother manual?"

"Betty Crocker."

"I feel like I'm going under a spell, Simon, not coming out of one."

"But what happens next? I wake up to find you gone, and I'm the pathetic pumpkin. Nothing left of you but broken glass."

"You've got it backward. We start as glass and a pumpkin. Then we wake up."

"So I'm a squash."

"Mmhm, one of those jack-o-lanterns left on the stoop too long, with a scowly face, all rotting and caving in. Until..." Indigo's fingers tip-toed up Simon's chest.

"I collapse."

"Unless…"

"A teenager smashes me in the street."

"You're hopeless." Indigo's laugh cut through Simon like light slicing through fog. "No, a confused boy in disguise walks up and fills you with candy. Until you're overflowing, and brimming, and stuffed."

"A stuffed squash. Thanks."

Indigo unzipped Simon's jeans and parted the fly, unhitching his cock from white briefs. "A crookneck squash, I'd say." He ran his soft palm along the bent shaft. His eyes widened as Simon's erection continued to grow in his palm. "A zucchini that gets left way too long in the garden."

Simon seized Indigo's wrist, though stopping him was one of the hardest things he'd done. "Let's throw a ball. Here. Tomorrow night. I'll clean the place up. Fix the jukebox. Invite some fairies and fag hags. I want you to see what this place can be."

"It's complicated, Simon. I'm on tour. I'm supposed to be in Columbus or some land-locked hellhole next. Where am I, anyway?"

Simon named the town, and because few had ever heard of it, named the closest inland city.

"That's not possible. I was hundreds of miles north of here. No wonder it's so much warmer."

"I think you're confused with all the traveling you must do. Anyway, what does it fucking matter if mermaids or mystical currents or Moby Dick himself carried you here if you're just going to leave?" Simon removed Indigo's hand from his cock and packed himself back away.

"I'll come back. I promise."

"Right. Like in a hundred years." He collected Indigo's coat from behind the bar and held it out for him. He'd guessed right. Indigo would never be seen with him with the doors thrown open. And he'd rather wander his arid dunes alone than with masked lovers who demanded his silence.

Indigo padded behind him. He moved with ease despite his sore foot, his legs long and nude under the big shirt. "That pesky rabbit's in the squash patch again."

Simon dropped the coat on the floor. "Shoot it. Put it out of its misery. Make a hell of a stew."

Indigo scrounged a pen from behind the bar and scrawled on an order pad. "Look. Tomorrow's headline." *Indigo Bleuz Suffers Laryngitis, Cancels World Tour!*

"I'm impressed. You spelled laryngitis correctly."

Indigo wriggled the tip of his nose like a rabbit. "Try again, Thumper."

"How'd you do that?" Simon tried to isolate just his nose tip to wiggle, but his whole face waggled with it. He went cross-eyed staring down at his large schnozz.

"I'm a man of many talents." Indigo picked up the note and held it in front of Simon's face. "You're hurting my feelings, though I'm well aware this stalling is a byproduct of those barnacles of yours."

Simon stared at the words Indigo had written, which blurred as he allowed himself to understand their import. "You'd do that for me?"

"I don't need millions anymore, Simon. Just one. Just you."

"Kinda stinks being a mere mortal."

"It's all I've ever been."

"I couldn't let you even *pretend* to give up your voice in order to be with me."

"Then come with me."

Simon shook his head. He would be a laughingstock, out among the glitterati and paparazzi. A Percheron lumbering amongst sleek polo ponies. "I know better than to leave my element. Look how it turned out for Rusalka. No, I'll wait for you here." He grabbed his long raincoat and tucked it around Indigo's shoulders. "Come on. I want to show you something." Indigo, who leapt like a dolphin through Simon's battered armor, would appreciate the sight of the aurora-worshipping porpoises. And whatever else might be out there.

Simon carried Indigo through a misty half-light across the deserted street. Such an easy weight in his arms. The unbuttoned flannel shirt had slipped off Indigo's shoulders and hung low behind him from his forearms like a wedding train. Indigo cuddled close and tongued Simon's ear, toyed with the hair—a few of them gone white—at the nape of Simon's neck. Anyone could see them, Simon knew, but Indigo didn't seem to care.

Dark rain clouds scuttled toward the horizon, and they reached the sea beneath a swath of clear sky, as if a hand had wiped a fogged window silvering above them. Simon dropped the coat onshore and lay Indigo down in the shallow, incoming surf. The shirt skirted around him in the water. Simon pulled it off and let it float away as he watched the waves lick at Indigo's legs.

Indigo shivered and reached for him. "What are you looking at?"

"To see if you turn into something else."

"Look. I am."

Indigo's cock yawned and stretched, rising toward the dawn. The ascending sun coroneted his blue-black hair, iridescent and alive in the waves that lapped around him. Morning's first blush tinted his cheeks. His nipples shone like oil slicks in the foam.

Simon spread the coat in a lee amidst driftwood logs and lay Indigo down. He whispered, "You go and sing. I'll wait for you. Just remember you promised to come back to me." He thought of the prince who cut through a murderous, spiked forest to reach his spellbound beloved. Indigo had hacked through Simon's thorns, and he believed that Indigo would return. Letting him go would be more difficult than withdrawing his claws, but the last thing Simon wanted was to silence the voice that had woken him, the most beautiful voice on earth.

"Every note I sing will be for you. Promise you'll wait for me." Indigo reached down and unhitched Simon's erection again. "Damn that's an overripe *eggplant*." Simon pulled a condom from his wallet, so crumpled he couldn't read the expiration date if he tried. Why he'd carried it all this time, he didn't know; he hardly ever threw wood, except his waking woody, much less met anyone he'd want to use it with. Yeah, probably expired, but hells bells there was only so much to be expected of a man when he was presented with a lover like this, so it would have to do. He lowered himself between Indigo's legs. He was moving too quickly, he knew, but Christgodalmighty he needed to be joined with this man, who'd made it clear he'd done it all before and knew what he was doing.

Indigo gasped, "No."

"You're shitting me." So close, it was hard to stop himself. He could continue. Indigo would not be able to stop him. Maybe Indigo didn't want him to. "You said you never say no." Wray had said no but meant yes. Indigo had seemed different.

"Shh. Shh." Indigo touched his lips. "I mean no rubber. You don't need it. I got tested so often I was practically anemic. And, since then, there hasn't been…" he trailed off. "I want to feel you. I want to feel you inside me. All of you. I want to feel you coming."

Of course Indigo was safe. No human disease could sully a magical being. "But you don't know about me." Simon knew he was safe, though. Wray had insisted on tests, since protection didn't factor into his fantasies of being forced, and there'd been no one since him.

"I trust you." He pulled the condom off Simon, nearly making Simon come right there in his hand. "Jeans, too. And those adorable tighty-whities." He yanked them down.

"No one's called anything about me adorable before." Simon kicked free of his clothes and threw them up over a log where they'd stay dry as the tide came in. He pushed toward Indigo again.

Indigo stopped him again. "Wait. I lied again."

"I'm not adorable?"

"No. Yes. I mean no, that's not what I lied about and yes you're adorable. Well, *that's* not adorable." He reached down and hefted the purple weight of Simon's erection. "Everything else, yes. But I need you to know something first."

Simon sagged in defeat. "You're not coming back. I know it."

"I am." Indigo grabbed a fistful of Simon's hair with his free hand and looked into Simon's mahogany eyes. "But I haven't done everything like I said. I've never let a man do this before. Everything else, but not this. And when I've let men touch me, I was fucked up. Drugs or booze or just plain out of my mind."

"You want me to stop?" It was half question, half bark. It would be almost impossible to stop now that Simon was this far, this aroused, Indigo's hand still on his shaft as it pressed against the opening to Indigo's core, right against the tight threshold; one small thrust and he'd be in. He hadn't been so aroused in…maybe ever. But he would stop, dammit, if that's what Indigo wanted. He wouldn't force Indigo or even pretend to. Wray had refused a safe word, wanted no way to change his mind, wanted to believe afterward that he'd been fucked against his will.

"No. I want it. All of it. But only from you. I want you to look at me. At *me*. To see me. I'll never be more real than this. I'm going to feel you, Simon. I'm going to feel all of it, and Christ there's a lot of it to feel. I haven't had anything but the hay or whatever it is that tea was made from. I know exactly what I'm doing." He pulled Simon down to his face and kissed him, pushing up and against Simon with his body, hand still on Simon's cock, urging him in.

Instead Simon licked his finger and reached down to slip it up Indigo's hole, finding no resistance. He played with it as they kissed.

Indigo tilted his body up to Simon's cock, which pulsed and twitched in Indigo's guiding hand. "Now, Simon."

One more finger.

"Simon, now."

One more.

"GoddamnitSimonnow. You. *Now.*"

So different from *no.* "Why do I think you're used to getting your own way all the time?" But Simon himself needed their union of bodies just as desperately, as immediately. He released his fingers and pushed slowly inside Indigo with his spit-lubed cock. "What's your name?" he breathed out.

Indigo gasped and bucked. "You forgot? Shitfuck." He grunted and grabbed Simon behind the neck with both hands, lifting his face to Simon's throat, biting and talking at the same time. "You're telling me you forgot my name while you're making love to me?" He threw his head back, then pulled himself up into another deep kiss, urging Simon's cock farther into him with his body. "No wonder you're alone," he mouthed into Simon's lips so that Simon could feel his mirthful smile. "More," he said.

69

"I don't want to hurt you." Simon looked down at him.

"More. Now."

"You never told me your name." Simon pushed in farther. "Your real name."

"Indigo's my legal name now."

"Sweet Jesus, you sure you've never done this before?" Indigo was open, open and trusting and slick and relaxed and urging him in, all of him, drawing him deeper, legs now locked behind Simon's back.

"I'm not Jesus, though some seem to think I am."

"Your real name, tell me."

"It's plain. Common." For the first time, Simon saw fear in his eyes. Fear that the spell he'd cast around himself would be broken and that with the revelation of his name, he'd become ordinary. Unwanted.

"You're extraordinary, and I want to say your name. Trust me."

"Rumpelstiltskin?"

Simon abruptly pulled out. It was maybe the most difficult thing he'd ever done. Indigo cried out. Simon bent down and took Indigo's cock down his throat.

"Not that. Please not that." Indigo arched, hands pulling Simon's hair hard. "Everybody wants that. I want...stop," he panted. "I want to come with you inside me. Please, I've never felt this empty. It's like you backed a fucking freighter out of the slip. Come back. Come back to me."

Garbled sounds from Simon were clearly another demand for Indigo's name. Simon knew he could wait. He would wait for as long as it took Indigo to tell him.

"I'll tell you. Be part of me again and I'll tell you."

Simon raised himself and Indigo guided his cock back inside him. Slowly, slowly, Simon filled Indigo's body, and Indigo arched up to meet him, coming as he whispered his name into Simon's ear. Simon groaned with the clenching and bucking of this beautiful body around him and he too came, moaning Indigo's real name. He was immediately hard again.

"My squash blossom." Indigo hummed as their bodies remained joined, Simon as slow and gentle in his lovemaking as Indigo's kiss. He kissed his humming into Simon's mouth, singing down into Simon's larynx, singing silver into his body. "My velveteen rabbit, my beautiful beast."

Pulling out of the kiss and looking down at his lover, Simon saw his own joy refracted back. No one had ever looked back at him like that before, with trust, not dread-mixed lust. Emotions played across Indigo's once-remote face, a mirror's splintered pieces falling back into place.

Simon heard something, just beyond the human spectrum of sound; he felt the pressure of it in his eardrums like when he dove too deep, and he knew the notes were in harmony with Indigo's song. And upon Simon's broad back he felt eyes, dancing across the waves that now fingered their feet.

"I didn't know that was even possible," Indigo crooned, so low Simon wouldn't have heard him if they weren't so close.

"Thought only some girls had G-spots. You made me come from touching me on the inside. That was...*intense*."

"Doesn't always happen that way."

"That crooked divining rod of yours took a bend in the road and found an erogenous zone I didn't know I had."

"But you're not gay. And you're not bi. And it's apparent you're not straight. What are you, then?"

"Yours. Stay inside me," Indigo whispered, pulling Simon's head down to his chest. "Stay inside me forever."

Simon rolled onto his back and pulled Indigo on top of him, cocooning the coat around him, and Indigo drowsed, sighing, as Simon rocked inside and around him. Wray had never fallen asleep afterward; he'd always showered and left.

Simon tried to stay hard, but when Indigo shifted in his embrace, Simon came again: a long, deep, slow convulsion. The incoming tide tongued their legs in the same leisurely rhythm.

Indigo's eyes fluttered open and a smile flirted with his lips. "That was nice," he murmured into Simon's nipple. "Like...hot chicken soup on a drizzly day. Served with a big spoon. A gravy ladle."

"Is that a compliment?" Simon growled. "Sounds grandmotherly."

Indigo took Simon's hand and lowered it down to his hard cock. "What do you think?" He groaned as Simon stroked him. "More like the big bad wolf."

"I want you inside me," Simon said, surprising himself. It was not unheard of for him, but certainly Wray had never topped him. "This, between us, has to be equal."

Indigo gazed up at him ruefully. "The fact that you're hung like a rhino makes equality impossible. Not that mine is anything to sneeze at. Or so I've been told. But I'm out of the running on girth. You can take my word on that since at the moment I'm measuring yours with the most delicate of gauges."

Simon sat up. "Yours is perfect." He stretched his arms wide. "Not too big." He held up thumb and forefinger. "Not too small." He pulled out of Indigo and slipped Indigo's cock into his mouth and down his throat, lubing him up well and mumbling three syllables, which Indigo understood as, "But juuuuust right." He worked Indigo until he was hard and wet and on the brink, with no protest this time, and then sat up and turned himself onto all fours in the sand and shallow water. That would be easiest for Indigo; Simon wasn't as flexible as this graceful muse. He faced the water, reaching back to guide Indigo inside him. "Beast," Indigo hummed, up on his knees, letting Simon guide him. "My beast, my very own beast." Then he shifted, snarling off the end of his song, pressing his chest to Simon's back and biting his shoulder, bucking hard behind him. He reached around to Simon's cock and worked him expertly, still biting, thrusting, insisting, beating Simon off with his smooth, elegant hand.

Simon wouldn't have thought he could come a third time; he was no spring chicken and had left his horny teens well back in the last century. But Christalmighty he was coming again. He reached down between his legs and grabbed Indigo's balls and slipped his middle finger into Indigo's ass, rubbing his fingers and palm against Indigo's taint and balls, pressing on his perineum. Indigo froze, as if stunned, and Simon felt the ejaculate pulse beneath his fingers before he felt warmth surge inside him. Indigo pushed deep into him and milked Simon's cock with his hand, and Simon let loose into the hissing foam of an incoming wave.

The sea caressed Simon's hand in the water. He looked down at his reflection and for a moment didn't recognize himself. Something darted under it under the water and his reflection rippled away.

"The fuck were you doing down there with your hand?" Indigo hugged Simon, his chest and cheek to Simon's back.

"I've got my secrets for letting the genie out of the lamp."

"Should be illegal. Or trademarked. You could franchise workshops and make a fortune while making the world a happier place. That was, that was all *amazing*." He kissed Simon's shoulder blade. "Did I hurt you?"

"Shouldn't I be asking you that?"

"Nah, apparently I like a big serving of ratatouille. Damn, check out these haunches of yours. All muscle. Like the Terminator."

"Sorry. Intimidating?"

"No, gorgeous. Fucking artwork. I'm going to commission a sculpture." Indigo admired Simon's ass and thighs with his hands.

"The only sculpture should be of you. Now move away from there before I throw you off."

"My shy, modest beast." Indigo flopped down into the water beside him. He floated on his back, feet toward shore. He bobbed on the mild, incoming waves, hair fanned around him. "Does anyone else even live in this town? Or is it some enchanted stronghold where everyone else is sleeping it off for a century?"

"They only come out once the Starbucks opens. We've got a while yet." Simon also knew the town cop, biblically speaking, from long ago, and the good officer had turned an occasional blind eye, and even chose to participate on certain skinny dipping occasions—God those were the good old days…had Simon once had carefree fun like that?

Simon sat back with a heavy splash, sitting up to his waist in the water, facing the horizon. He'd be sorry for that move when he found himself still leaking sand a few days later. He took hold of Indigo's ankles and steered him so that Indigo's knees were under his arms. Indigo naturally hooked his ankles behind Simon's back. Indigo's hair spread in a plume on the water. His arms floated out wide and he was humming again.

"You even have sexy underarms," Simon mused. "How is that even fair?"

"I have something else I need to confess."

Simon bent over and sucked on Indigo's kneecap. "And knees, too. Sculpted knees." He lifted the leg to tongue behind the knee.

"I've defiled a classic or two."

"You're making up for it with whatever that is you're singing. What is it?"

"Don't know. Just entered my head. Could be the first decent thing I've come up with in a while."

Simon felt that pressure in his eardrums again. "Maybe you're taking dictation." He licked the salt from Indigo's inner thigh.

"Songwriting feels like that sometimes. Never as strong as tonight, though. I'm just following along with the things you're doing to me down there. I might get jealous if I knew how many lucky fellows you've practiced those piano-hand moves on."

"Not really any. I'm not terribly dexterous. I'm just following along with your song."

"Think I'll call it Cottontail in the Deflowers." Indigo floated and hummed, then paused and spoke to the sky. "Simon?"

"Mm?"

"Could you do that again? That thing with your fingers?"

"Well aren't *we* insatiable?" Simon pulled him gently closer but used his tongue instead between Indigo's spread legs.

"So's I don't forget the song. Besides, I think you're still one ahead of me and you said we had to keep this even."

"That I did." Simon vibrated his low murmur through the recesses of Indigo's body.

"Yeah. Like that. Oh."

Simon could have sucked on Indigo's balls and taint and hole and cock all day, all seasoned with salt water, except that then he couldn't watch the pleasure he gave reflected in Indigo's beautiful face. He switched to using his fingers, using his other hand to play the outside of Indigo's body.

Indigo sang.

Ripples plinked the surface near Indigo's head. Too big for fish.

Simon couldn't see his own cock under the water, under Indigo's body, but the rippling current of the incoming tide played against his entire package like a mouth.

Indigo's head should have been dipping beneath the surface, he should have been taking water into his mouth and nose, but it was as if something were buoying him up from beneath.

The sun rose fully above the horizon, breaking open the sky, and something washed over Indigo's belly, a mass of seaweed like a head of tangled hair. Indigo's note descended a guttural octave as he came into whatever it was, Simon, too, coming into the mouth of current beneath him.

In a flash, Simon saw two men, long-haired, standing in the breakers, cocks in each other's hands, kissing deeply. They stroked each other's cocks quickly, furiously, as though in a race against time, and he witnessed the unmistakable buck and quake of their bodies as they came, and then they slipped beneath the surface and were gone.

"Thank you," he said to the horizon, and his old chums the dolphins erupted up into the full sun, leaping and dancing.

Indigo sat up and pulled himself into Simon's lap. "Don't thank me. I should be thanking you. Christ, how did you do that? It was like you had four hands and two mouths."

"Magic."

"Man I like this place."

Simon pointed to the dolphins. "Look."

Indigo hummed his new wordless song, and the dolphins moved toward shore. Simon had never seen them this close. They chirped and clicked and slapped their flippers and flukes on the water, as if they were chatting with Indigo. And then they were gone. "What were you saying to them?" Simon asked.

"Asking them to take care of you while I'm gone. And to turn you to stone if you so much as look at another man. Now that would be one hell of a statue."

Simon rested his chin on Indigo's head, holding him tight in his arms. "I never understood how they could be so joyous just because of the break of day. Now I understand." But a note of sadness crept into his voice. "Tell me what it's going to be like when you come back. What if the bar's packed with customers? Would you want to be seen there?" He reached for the half-wet coat behind them and draped it over his shoulders, drawing it around them more to shield Indigo than himself. The skirt hem swanned on the dancing water.

"Is it ever packed, Simon?"

"It will be. You'll see. I'm going to make it what I once envisioned. What it once was. But I promise the camera will still be broken."

"Had a sneaking suspicion it wasn't working. But I'd trust you even if it was. Maybe I'd even like watching a recording of us, so I could figure out the secret of what you do down there."

"Then I'd have to take your firstborn, I'm afraid."

He nipped at Simon's nipple. "Well, this is what's going to happen. One day you're going to look up, and you're going to see a white stretch limo parked out at the curb."

"Not glass?"

"Not enough privacy. And the driver will come into the bar and sit down, and you'll set an overflowing beer in front of him, no charge. Then you'll come outside and climb in the back of the limo, and I'll be waiting."

"So you won't have to be seen with me in a gay bar?"

"Because if I walk into the bar and see you after being apart, I'll cream my jeans."

"Are you going to be dressed, in the back of that limo?"

"Mm…yes. I'll be in a white tuxedo. Which won't be on for long, at least the bottom half, because I'll be so hungry for that crookneck squash of yours that I'll lap-dance you while we kiss and drink champagne."

"You don't care that everyone will see the limo bouncing on its tires?" Simon pictured his big palms on Indigo's waist under his shirttails as he thrust up ardently into him.

"You have more class than that, Simon—you'd spill the champagne," Indigo teased. "And this is going to be the good stuff, the best I can find for you."

"Save your money. I'd be happy with a Guinness. As long as it came with a serving of you."

"And just like pouring a Guinness, you're going to go slow."

"It'll be tough after not seeing you." But picturing the languid, languorous movements of Indigo, straddling him on white leather seats, turned him on more than the flash he'd had of an urgent, quick coupling.

"And then we'll spruce ourselves up a bit, and you'll take me by the hand into your bar, and put some Sinatra on the jukebox, and you'll dance with me." Indigo nuzzled against him.

"I don't dance."

"You'll move slowly and erotically with me in your arms and press your crotch insistently into my pelvis."

"Can do."

"Then, when I'm turned on again so bad I can't stand it, which should take about half of a standard three-minute Blue Eyes tune, you'll take me back into your stockroom or walk-in refrigerator or the john or wherever…"

"My bedroom's right upstairs."

"Too far. This time we'll go faster. You'll have me singing so loud that everyone will know I'm yours. And then you can take me back out into the bar and give me a cup of that magic straw tea of yours, and I bet nobody will bug me with you giving them the evil eye. And you'll feed me, because we'll have a long night ahead of us."

"I'm going to fatten you up beyond recognition, my pretty."

"And I'll cop a feel whenever you pass me, which you'll do more often than you need to, and then you'll kick everybody out and you'll get me out of my tux and bend me over a stool and do that thing that you're doing right now." He purred into Simon's neck.

Simon indeed had nudged Indigo's thighs apart and had his hands between them again. He couldn't help himself. "Not bent over the barstool. I want to see your face. Just like now. Right here on the beach." He understood that was part of the bargain he'd struck, and it was no hardship: the gift that kept on giving, as was the way with true love. "And then I carry you to a proper mattress. No peas."

"I'm painting it the way I see it. You asked."

"I just wanted to know if I was supposed to pretend not to know you. I don't want to blow your image."

"The only image I care about is the one I see in front of me right now." He looked at Simon's face. He hiccupped. "Simon, what are you doing down...?" He moaned. "*More* tricks?"

"Imagine what I could do with sleeves." Simon's hand splashed the water. "*Simon Says...*" he trailed off.

"Yeah. That. There. *That.*"

"I've never ridden in a limo before."

"I like it that I'll give you something you've never had before." Indigo panted out the words.

"You already are."

J.D. Romann

Acknowledgments

Thank you to these editors who believed in the work of an unknown author and first published these stories: Nick Street, Jesse Grant, Michael Huxley, Sean Meriwether, and Jamie Joy Gatto.

Thank you to my lifelong partner for loving me despite my spending so much time with other, albeit fictional, men. None of them come close to how sexy you are.

Thanks to tremendous friends Jackson Lassiter (Birds of a Feather: Short Stories and Personal Essays Inspired by a Gay Life), Maureen O'Donnell (Scar Flowers), and Maria Elena de la Selva (Best Women's Erotica), who gave me invaluable feedback on these stories. Also thanks to Hydra House Books.

Thank you to the readers who took a chance on this small collection. I am honored that you chose to spend your time and money on this book. If you liked it, please consider leaving a review. Positive reviews are a huge help to indie authors and are much appreciated.

More J.D. Romann titles will be available soon. If you would like to receive an email when new titles are released, please send an email to JDRomann@hotmail.com. You will receive very few emails, and your address will not be shared. Visit www.JDRomann.com for information and updates on new releases.

About the Author

J.D. Romann's stories have been published in two editions of *Best Gay Love Stories*; *Friction (Best Gay Erotic Fiction)*; *Wet Nightmares, Wet Dreams (Literotica)*; *VelvetMafia.com*, and *MindCaviar.com (Food, Sex, Literature, Art)*. Her alter-ego has been published in two editions of *Best American Erotica*, seven editions of *Mammoth Book of Best New Erotica*, *Best Women's Erotica*, and many other places. Born and raised in Hawaii, J.D. lived for a time in New Orleans, where she was given all the worldly possessions of an obsessed serial killer fan who mysteriously disappeared. She still has that creepy suitcase, among other things, in her closet. She now lives in the gray and moldy Pacific Northwest, where her imagination continues to provide a match for her reality. She once watched a Slash concert at the old Fenix Underground in Pioneer Square, where she was mesmerized by Slash's burning lock of hair that he never noticed. She loves her red shit-kickers. She was raised by an English teacher, and she is a freelance editor whose motto is, "Grammar and spelling errors are boner-killers."

www.ingramcontent.com/pod-product-compliance
Lightning Source LLC
Chambersburg PA
CBHW020337290526
45785CB00005B/2068